Reflections on
'A Course in Miracles'

Reflections on
' A Course in Miracles'

VOLUME ONE

STEPHANIE PANAYI

BubbaChi Press

First published by BubbaChi Press 2019

First edition

ISBN: 978-0-646-80900-7

Typeset by Reedsy

Contents

Preface

In March of 2019 I published my first book, *Above the Battleground: The Courageous Path to Emotional Autonomy and Inner Peace*. The book was the result of seven years of research and pondering, combining elements of traditional psychoanalytic thought with principles from *A Course in Miracles*. Having completed the book I found I still had many ideas floating about which — though they didn't make it past the cutting room floor — still grabbed my attention for one reason or another. This led to the birth of my blog, 'Reflections on *A Course in Miracles*'.

Each essay seeks to relate principles from the Course to practical living, and often incorporates the thoughts of philosophers and the like that I have found intriguing. I have arranged them in chronological order from the oldest to most recent, and I hope that you find them useful.

1

Resilience and a Secure Base

W hat makes us resilient in the face of difficult circumstances? What 'steadies our nerves' and helps us deal with the unexpected, the incomprehensible and the strange?

John Bowlby's attachment theory suggests that a secure attachment to a parent during childhood is a major contributor to resilience. Bowlby was a British psychologist who found that a child with secure attachment is less likely to experience separation anxiety when the parent is absent, and more likely to embrace novel situations without fear. This sense of security developed as the child felt loved and supported — comforted in times of distress and also encouraged to explore their freedom as the need arose. In this way, a parent provides a secure base, a haven to which a child knows they can return. According to this theory, the child progressively internalises the external secure base, leading to more resilience in the face of calamity, misfortune and uncertainty.

For people growing up without such a secure base, challenging circumstances can produce extreme anxiety — there is a sense of vulnerability associated with 'going it alone'. Indeed, one of the reasons it's widely accepted that the relationship between therapist and client is the most potent source of healing, is that the therapist provides that secure base for the client. The client learns that the therapist is there for them, won't abandon them, and so they internalise a sense of value and security.

A Secure Base, ACIM-Style

Two major themes running through the Teacher's Manual of *A Course in Miracles* (ACIM) are the importance of seeing shared interests and of asking for help from our internal Teacher. In the spirit of attachment theory, following these two principles provides us with a secure base in times of trouble and despair.

The principle of shared interests means that despite all of our apparent differences — physical, ideological, financial — we are all the same in sharing the one need to awaken to our inherent wholeness/holiness, and the same source of despair — the belief that we have separated from Love and the security of Home.

In times of distress, it's tempting to focus on how we think others are making things worse for us, and this usually relates to how they are doing things we wouldn't do, behaving in ways we wouldn't behave, even liking things we don't like. We see our differences, we compare and contrast; we *judge*. This increases our anxiety because making differences a big deal reinforces our belief in separation from our Source (Heaven is an undifferentiated unity). As our anxiety increases so too does our reflexive need to blame it on something or someone outside ourselves, and a vicious cycle ensues.

To look upon someone as we would look upon ourselves — as having the same fears and need, despite our differences in form — is therefore a key to resilience. The principle of sameness/shared interests reflects the truth of our oneness. We can't, however, make this shift in perspective on our own because we are so wedded to judging based on the form of people's behaviour — on what they say, do, or don't do. To be able to allow the idea of sameness to take hold we need help from our inner Teacher — what ACIM refers to as the Holy Spirit, the link to the truth of Who we are and of our eternal safety and worthiness. Asking for help creates an open-mindedness that allows our inner Teacher to touch us with the reality of our sameness and at the same time answer our need to feel supported.

It's important, therefore, not to get lost in the seeming enormity of external challenges and forget the mindful steps we can take to develop resilience. All circumstances are the same in that they offer us the same opportunity to remember shared interests with everyone we encounter and to call upon help to do this. If I'm going through a difficult divorce for example, I can focus on it as the main source of my despair and its resolution as my only source of hope, forgetting that *every* circumstance (from interactions at the grocery store to how we perceive someone on television) offers me an opportunity to ask for help to remember sameness, and therefore to feel better. It's by making this process a habit of mind that we shore-up our resilience and establish a secure base from which to meet the world.

2

A Western Yoga

'Yoga' is Sanskrit for 'to yoke'; to bring together or connect. Mindfully employing specific physical postures — what we commonly know as yoga — has been used for centuries in the East to help produce a peaceful state of mind connecting the practitioner to their divine nature.

A Course in Miracles could likewise be regarded as a form of yoga: applying its principles of forgiveness (mindfully working with our psychological body) helps remove the obstacles to peace, connecting us with our transcendent Self.

Wings to Prayer

A Course in Miracles offers a two-pronged approach to inner peace: forgiveness and prayer. A beautiful passage from the *Song of Prayer* pamphlet explains how forgiveness and prayer are allies in our quest for peace:

Forgiveness offers wings to prayer, to make its rising easy and its progress swift. Without its strong support it would be vain to try to rise above prayer's bottom step, or even to attempt to climb at all. Forgiveness is prayer's ally; sister in the plan for your salvation. Both must come to hold you up and keep your feet secure; your purpose steadfast and unchangeable. Behold the greatest help that God ordained to be with you until you reach to Him. Illusion's end will come with this (S-2.In.1:1-6).

Forgiveness — recalling our projected guilt — requires a willingness to be wrong ('I'm never upset for the reason I think'); and prayer — asking for help — requires humility:

Prayer is a way to true humility. And here again it rises slowly up, and grows in strength and love and holiness. Let it but leave the ground where it begins to rise to God, and true humility will come at last to grace the mind that thought it was alone and stood against the world (S-1.V.1:1-3).

The ultimate in prayer is pure communion with the divine, but this is something we reach gradually alongside our progression with forgiveness. The Course emphasises that though God can be reached directly, such awareness can only occur once the barriers of our guilt have been removed. Forgiveness is the process of doing this — it is the indirect means for knowing God; for *meeting the conditions* of knowledge:

This course will lead to knowledge, but knowledge itself is still beyond the scope of our curriculum... The readiness for knowledge still must be attained (T-18.IX.11:1,7).

Acceptance of our guiltlessness is the condition for knowing God, and we become aware of our guiltlessness as we withdraw our projected guilt from others, address our feelings of victimisation, and ask for help to see things differently — from the perspective of the Holy Spirit who knows of our innocence, wholeness and invulnerability. Indeed, when we accept our guiltlessness (the Atonement principle) we'll know we 'need do nothing' for our salvation and that there is no need for time:

'I need do nothing' is a statement of allegiance, a truly undivided loyalty. Believe it for just one instant, and you will accomplish more than is given to a century of contemplation, or of struggle against temptation... Here is the quick and open door through which you slip past centuries of effort, and escape from time.. (T-18.VII.6:7-8;7:3).

The following dream illustrates the helping hand that forgiveness provides for us along our ultimate path to communion with God:

I was standing in a large church-like room with rows of seating facing the entrance. The main feature of the room was a narrow mezzanine floor with a balustrade high on the opposite wall. To the right of the mezzanine was an ancient-looking stone staircase leading up to it. The stairs were uneven and dented, and the staircase itself was extremely steep.

An elderly woman holding a book entered the room and headed straight for the staircase. She took a few steps up and I could see that she was struggling. Concerned for her welfare I suggested that she stop climbing but she said she needed to return the book at the mezzanine. I told her I would return it for her, and led her to a seat where she sat, utterly exhausted, facing the entrance.

Looking towards the mezzanine I noticed another point of access to it on the left — a series of gently inclined ramps arranged in a zigzag pattern. Taking this gentler route I easily arrived at the mezzanine floor. The wall was lined with Buddhist artifacts and Eastern books on spirituality. An elderly man was standing there to receive the book I was returning, and a Buddhist monk was asleep on the floor. I was concerned I might wake him, but the elderly man said there was little chance of that, and then I myself awoke.

The gently inclined ramps represented the opportunities for forgiveness that help raise us to meet our goal; the ultimate object of our prayers. But trying to reach 'Heaven' directly, as by the steep but direct stone staircase, is incredibly arduous. Why? Because while we seek for communion yet hold onto our guilt and unforgiveness we are working against ourselves. Indeed, our exhaustion can be so great that we need to 'turn our backs' on the whole process for a while (hence the seats facing away from the mezzanine floor).

It's important, then, not to trivialise the importance of looking at our ego in order to transcend it — this emphasis is why the Course can be regarded as a truly psycho-spiritual text, and forgiveness a form of yoga bridging our earthly experience as an individual with our eternal reality as spirit.

3

Loneliness

L oneliness isn't simply a numbers game. We can be alone but not lonely; we can be in the company of friends and yet feel isolated. What, then, is at the heart of a painfully lonely experience?

The subject of loneliness came to the fore for me several years ago via a dream:

I was walking out of a university building having finished studying all that I could there, yet I was plagued by a sense that something important was missing. As I walked across the campus I saw a two-storey building within the university grounds, separate from the main facilities. A large wooden cross was atop the building and the exterior ground-level walls were made of glass. A series of abstract paintings, largely of red, orange and yellow hues, were displayed on this floor as if it was a gallery.

I was intrigued and drawn to this building. As I approached its main face I was met with an external staircase leading to the second floor. There was no entrance at ground-level, so I climbed the stairs and opened a door at the top landing. Inside was a large room full of people walking around, and I felt that the setting was a psychology tutorial. Surveying the scene I noticed people in different states of despair. One person was delusional, gesticulating to the walls and empty space, another was filled with anguish as someone emotionally close to them walked out of the room. I felt the pain of this second person's loss, and as I did a white-haired man appeared at my side and asked me the following question:

'If you could use one word to describe the source of all of these people's distress, what would it be?'

For a moment I was puzzled. I had no clue as to what the answer could be, but in another moment I knew the answer without question:

'Loneliness', I replied.

'That's right', he said, to my relief — I felt like I had passed a test.

The white-haired psychologist then moved to one end of the room and began to give a lesson on loneliness. He wrote four letters on a huge blackboard: A, B, C, D. After speaking about each of these letters his subject broadened (I can't remember the details). I considered taking down notes but decided not to since I'd noticed a class manual on a table beside me and assumed all the details would be in there.

As the psychologist rounded off his presentation, I turned to the manual and saw the title 'Transpersonal Psychology' on the cover. I opened it and found, to my horror, that it didn't contain notes from the psychologist's speech at all, but pictures of sunsets, landscapes, and the occasional poem by the Sufi poet Rumi.

The dream's meaning became clear when I awoke. As part of my psychology and counselling training (in real life), the letters A, B, C, and D referred to four personality types I had studied. The psychologist's message was that loneliness was associated with not connecting with your true, 'authentic' self, nor with the transpersonal, ego-transcendent aspect of your being (as represented by the manual full of landscapes and inspired poetry).

Comparisons — The Home of Self-Doubt

We generally don't want to feel different when we're children — we seem to be inherently suspicious of differences rather than intrigued by them. To be different is often to be alone.

Children aren't born a blank slate — the ego thought system is as strong in them as in all of us, and their behaviour often highlights key elements of it that are operative in the well-socialised adult who nonetheless believes he or she is fair, kind, and tolerant. We mightn't act as readily on our comparisons, but compare we do.

Comparisons are the ego's 'daily bread' and are a major contributor to not being at peace with, or true to, ourselves. Hot on the heels of any comparison are the judgements of 'better' and 'worse' which increase our feelings of separation, loneliness and anxiety. And if we try to remove this anxiety by not being true to ourselves, this also leads to a sense of loneliness in unconscious recognition of the authentic self we've left behind. In order to feel free to be who we are — an A, B, C, or D-type for example — we need to be free of the anxiety that comes from emphasising differences.

The second component of our loneliness — a lack of communion with the Divine, or our transcendent Self — isn't possible to remedy while we entertain grievances. This is a major principle of the Course:

Communion is impossible alone. No one who stands apart can receive Christ's vision. It is held out to him, but he cannot hold out his hand to receive it (P-2.II.9:1-3).

The way to stand with another is to look beyond differences to our shared need:

Let him be still and recognize his brother's need is his own. And let him then meet his brother's need as his and see that they are met as one, for such they are. What is religion but an aid in helping him to see that this is so? (P-2.II.9:4-6)

Religion here refers to an experience, not to a formal religion, and any truly religious experience entails an appreciation of our connectedness. Regarding this experience, the ground-floor paintings in my dream reminded me of Mark Rothko's painting *Untitled (Red)*. I had seen it once at a gallery, and read that Rothko had hoped it conveyed the religious experience he had felt whilst creating it.

I find it interesting that the building in my dream couldn't be accessed at the 'religious experience' level — it formed the foundation for what was above, but couldn't be entered directly. Remembering our sameness — thereby feeling freer to be ourselves — and being open to commune with that which is invisible to the eye but known to the heart is the Course's path to religious experience.

4

Before the Dawn: Part One

W hile the Course contains some beautiful passages relating to 'love and light', it also describes the discomfort we are likely to encounter as we apply its principles of forgiveness. There are two major sources of this discomfort: resistance, and the thought reversal involved in accepting the Course's principles.

Resistance

The following words from the Song of Prayer pamphlet highlight the pain of looking at our guilt (the bedrock of the ego thought system) in order to relinquish our identification with it:

Guilt must be given up, and not concealed. Nor can this be done without some pain, and a glimpse of the merciful nature of this step may for some time be followed by a deep retreat into fear (S-1.III.4:1-2).

Of particular note in this passage are the words 'given up' – this implies that there is a part of us that wants to hold onto our guilt. Indeed, the Course talks of 'The hanging-on to guilt, its hugging-close and sheltering, its loving protection and alert defense...' (P-2.VI.1:3). Our attachment to guilt is why we find it difficult to forgive others – to withdraw our projections of guilt – and then to forgive ourselves.

The cause of our resistance is our attachment to the self we think we are and that we have identified with for so long. And just as it is difficult and painful to lose someone who has been close to us for many years, it is also painful to lose an identification that has provided a refuge. All of us think our ego-identification protects us in some way. Our ingrained defences and habits have been our chosen armour for getting by in the world.

We also don't want to lose our sense of specialness (even if it's a sense of being especially flawed, unworthy or sinful). The ego self – identified with the body – is separate from others, from God, and is unique. The pain of our grievances and self-accusations is more easily tolerated than we think because we're more afraid of the all-encompassing love of God that lies beyond them – we don't want to lose our ego self within an undifferentiated oneness; we want to stand out as something different. We are, in effect, afraid of our redemption:

You could look even upon the ego's darkest cornerstone without fear if you did not believe that, without the ego, you would find within yourself something you fear even more. You are not really afraid of crucifixion. Your real terror is of redemption...

You realize that, by removing the dark cloud that obscures it, your love for your Father would impel you to answer His Call and leap into Heaven. You believe that attack is salvation because it would prevent you from this (T-13.III.1:9-11;2:6-7).

Resistance and the Authority Problem

There is another element to our resistance, and that is our desire to be autonomous, to 'be the boss of us'. The perceived separation from God was partly brought about by our desire to be noticed as something apart from the All and partly by a wish to be our own authority – the essence of 'the authority problem':

The problem everyone must decide is the fundamental question of authorship. All fear comes ultimately, and sometimes by way of very devious routes, from the denial of Authorship. The offense is never to God, but only to those who deny Him. To deny His Authorship is to deny yourself the reason for your peace, so that you see yourself only in segments. This strange perception is the authority problem (T-3.VI.10:3-7).

We don't want to be restored to our 'proper place' because we think it would diminish us:

You have built your whole insane belief system because you think you would be helpless in God's Presence... You are afraid it would sweep you away from yourself and make you little, because you believe that magnitude lies in defiance, and that attack is grandeur (T-13.III.4:1-2).

A core ego principle is 'one or the other'. In order for me to have power in a relationship, the other person must have less power. Therefore, if we defer to God by being receptive to His Will, we think we have lost power. The reflection of God's Will for us in this world is to practice forgiveness, and so holding onto grievances and our guilt is a means of defiance. Indeed, we like the idea of our autonomy so much, that we'd prefer to do things on our own, in our own way, even if it hurts us.

But, as the Course states, though our tolerance for pain may be high, it's not without limit (T-2.III.3:5). To accept that God's Will for us is also our own – that forgiveness offers us everything we want (W-122) – is the way to accepting our true inheritance and true power, a power that is shared by everyone as being a part of Everything:

Who assumes a power that he does not possess is deceiving himself. Yet to accept the power given him by God is but to acknowledge his Creator and accept His gifts. And His gifts have no limit. To ask the Holy Spirit to decide for you is simply to accept your true inheritance (M-29.5:1-4).

A reflection of true power in this world is the ability to choose to listen to our inner Teacher whose lessons will lead us to a more consistent experience of peace not contingent on external circumstance. We shut God out by not listening to our inner Teacher and by judging others. Importantly, this doesn't mean that we should consciously pose a worded question to the Holy Spirit every time there is a decision to be made throughout the day. Indeed, this is likely to have a cramping effect on the mind which would hinder communication:

Does this mean that you cannot say anything without consulting Him? No, indeed! That would hardly be practical... If you have made it a habit to ask for help when and where you can, you can be confident that wisdom will be given you when you need it. Prepare for this each morning, remember God when you can throughout the day, ask the Holy Spirit's help when it is feasible to do so, and thank Him for His guidance at night. And your confidence will be well founded indeed (M-29.5:5-10).

Meister Eckhart, the fourteenth century Christian mystic, spoke of having an inner movement towards God, rather than constantly trying to use words to develop or maintain a connection. Likewise, the Course tells us to 'Never forget that the Holy Spirit does not depend on your words. He understands the requests of your heart, and answers them' (M-29.6:1-2).

The humility of our ego, then, is needed to help overcome our resistance. We need to be willing to 'choose the second place to gain the first' (W-328). We also need to develop trust that the process of forgiveness will truly give us what we want – that the pain of losing 'the devil we know' will be worth it. In part 2 of this article, we look at the discomfort caused by the thought reversal inherent in the forgiveness process.

5

Before the Dawn: Part Two

P art one of this article explored how resistance to losing our separate identity (our 'specialness'), and to losing our autonomy (being our own boss), make the process of undoing our ego-identification painful. Here in part two we explore another cause of our pain — the instability and confusion we encounter as we reverse the ego-based thinking that heretofore has guided our lives.

Thought Reversal

The ego thought system is based on separation, differences, and opposites, all of which relate to form – to what we can see, hear, feel, or touch. Another way of describing form is to say that it is specific. To specify something is to draw a boundary around it; to distinguish it from something else. In contrast to the ego's thought system, the Holy Spirit's is based on the reality of a formless, abstract unity in which 'nowhere does the Father end, the Son begin as something separate from Him' (W-132.12:4).

Since the foundations of these thought systems are poles apart, moving from an ego-orientation to a right-minded one will cause periods of instability and uncertainty as we change our 'upside-down' orientation:

As these false underpinnings are given up, the equilibrium is temporarily experienced as unstable. However, nothing is less stable than an upside-down orientation (T-1.V.6:5-6).

The thought reversal that causes us the most discombobulation involves the notions of giving and receiving. In the right-minded thought system, giving and receiving are the same. This principle is expressed in the Holy Spirit's lesson: 'To have, give all to all' (T-6.V.A.5:13). The Holy Spirit's lesson reflects the reality of an abstract oneness where what we give we must also receive, and this is true on the level of the mind outside time and space.

However, because we experience ourselves as a specific person in a specific body in a world of specifics, we believe that to give something is then to be without it — a fundamental principle within the ego thought system. We project our guilt onto someone else, for example, thinking that this rids us of it. The belief that we are essentially our (separate) bodies contributes to this, and so the idea that we are all one is difficult to grasp in any meaningful way:

One brother is all brothers. Every mind contains all minds, for every mind is one. Such is the truth. Yet do these thoughts make clear the meaning of creation? Do these words bring perfect clarity with them to you? What can they seem to be but empty sounds; pretty, perhaps, correct in sentiment, yet fundamentally not understood nor understandable. The mind that taught itself to think specifically can no longer grasp abstraction in the sense that it is all-encompassing. We need to see a little, that we learn a lot (W-161.4:1-8).

We connect with the truths that minds are joined and that giving and receiving are the same (we 'learn a lot') by practicing forgiveness with the specifics (jobs, partners, parents, children, friends, etc.) of our life:

Complete abstraction is the natural condition of the mind. But part of it is now unnatural. It does not look on everything as one. It sees instead but fragments of the whole... Thus were specifics made... And now it is specifics we must use in practicing (W-161.2:1;3:1-2).

It's through the process of forgiveness that we 'see a little': as we experience the peace that comes from giving forgiveness (rather than projecting guilt) in various relationships, we'll be able to generalise the lesson that to give and receive are the same — that to bless another is to bless ourselves in recognition of the holiness we share. In contrast, if we try to rid ourselves of our guilt by projecting it out, not only will the guilt remain ('Ideas leave not their source' [T-26.VII.4:7]) but we will have reinforced it because teaching and learning are the same:

When a brother behaves insanely, you can heal him only by perceiving the sanity in him. If you perceive his errors and accept them, you are accepting yours. If you want to give yours over to the Holy Spirit, you must do this with his... How is this different from telling you that what you teach you learn? (T-9.III.5:1-3;5).

Any situation must be to you a chance to teach others what you are, and what they are to you. No more than that, but also never less. (M-in.2:9-11).

If someone appears to act unkindly, for example, but we see beyond the behaviour to the thought of fear behind it and accept that they are still a part of Christ (not their ego, but their Self), we have learnt that our own mistakes have not affected our holiness.

Unholy Relationships and the Getting Concept

Another reason why the Holy Spirit's lesson, 'To have, give all to all', is a major departure from the ego thought system, is that it represents the first step in the undoing of 'the getting concept':

The ego never gives out of abundance, because it was made as a substitute for it. That is why the concept of 'getting' arose in the ego's thought system (T-4.II.7:3-4).

Believing we have left the totality of our Creator and lost the wholeness and abundance of our Self, we identify with deficiency and vulnerability and seek to make up for our perceived lack. The Course calls any relationship in which we try to get something to make up for feelings of insecurity an 'unholy' or 'special' relationship. It is special because it assumes that a particular person, activity or object can offer us something of more value than someone or something else. (If forgiveness is our goal, then every encounter is of equal value in that it offers us the same opportunity to practice forgiveness.)

We might seek for approval in intimate relationships, for example, to keep our sense of unworthiness at bay, and as long as a relationship seems to meet these needs it is filled with 'special love'. When our partner doesn't give us what we think we need, however, we project our hatred and guilt onto them and they become an object of 'special hate'. (*If only you'd give me what I want I could be happy!*)

When we've had enough of the pain inherent in the special love/hate relationship (for our ego needs can never be fully satisfied, our sense of incompleteness never repaired) and choose the Course's way forward, we won't be immediately met with rainbows and daffodils. On the contrary, we're likely to experience significant inner conflict due to the absolute thought reversal involved in our shift of purpose. We are changing our focus from meeting the defensive needs of our separate, specific, individual self, to meeting our shared need – to remember our holiness. In effect, our goal is shifting from what we can *get* from someone to what we *give* or 'teach' by way of our perceptions of them. With this shift in purpose, the relationship can for a while seem 'disturbed, disjunctive and even quite distressing' (T-17.V.3:3):

Be comforted in this; the only difficult phase is the beginning. For here, the goal of the relationship is abruptly shifted to the exact opposite of what it was. This is the first result of offering the relationship to the Holy Spirit, to use for His purposes...

In its unholy condition, your goal was all that seemed to give it meaning. Now it seems to make no sense. Many relationships have been broken off at this point, and the pursuit of the old goal re-established in another relationship (T-17.V.2:5-7;3:6-8).

What also adds to our difficulty is that often this shift seems to be induced by external circumstances that make pursuit of our former goals no longer viable. If, for example, the financial status of my partner provides me with a sense of status I crave but they unexpectedly lose their job and future work prospects, I can no longer depend on the relationship to meet this goal. What, then, is my goal for the relationship to be? As stated in the section 'The Development of Trust', how can we recognise the lack of value in ego goals unless we are in a position where we *must* see things differently? What induces us to trust that *forgiveness* will give us everything we want, rather than our special love bargains?

First, they must go through what might be called 'a period of undoing.' This need not be painful, but it usually is so experienced. It seems as if things are being taken away, and it is rarely understood initially that their lack of value is merely being recognized. How can lack of value be perceived unless the perceiver is in a position where he must see things in a different light? He is not yet at a point at which he can make the shift entirely internally. And so the plan will sometimes call for changes in what seem to be external circumstances. These changes are always helpful (M-4.I.A.3:1-7).

Instead of reinforcing my sense of insecurity and incompleteness by trying to get you to make up for them, I can learn of my innate abundance and wholeness by practicing forgiveness with you. Again, until we embrace the new goal — trusting that it will give us what we truly want — the situation is likely to be experienced as very dicey. 'This is the time for faith' we are told (T-17.V.6:1), for now the old goals to protect us from our insecurities are gone, the relationship can seem purposeless:

A sense of aimlessness will come to haunt you, and to remind you of all the ways you once sought for satisfaction and thought you found it. Forget not now the misery you really found, and do not breathe life into your failing ego. For your relationship has not been disrupted. It has been saved (T-17.V.8:3-6).

Instead of unconsciously bargaining with each other to meet our separate goals (to fulfil our defensive needs), we can now walk beside each other by realising our shared goal:

You are very new in the ways of salvation, and think you have lost your way. Your way is lost, but think not this is loss. In your newness, remember that you and your brother have started again, together (T-17.V.9:1-3).

It's not necessary for all parties to consciously be a partner in the forgiveness process for it to be effective. The dissociation from God 'is healed in both of you as you become aware of the Call for God in him, and thus acknowledge Its being' (T-5.III.2:10). To start again, together with our brother, means that we are no longer excluding them by seeing them as something separate that can fulfill our needs, but as someone whose holiness we share. It means we shift our focus from what we get from them (a smile, praise, disinterest, disapproval) to what we give (how we choose to perceive them).

In conclusion, a period of significant inner turbulence is incidental to the process of undoing our identification with the ego. Rather than a sign that things are falling apart (or that our spiritual aspirations have been misguided), feelings of instability, anxiety, anger and depression are familiar companions for those willing to endure the 180-degree shift in perspective that the Course's process of forgiveness initiates. We are assured, however, that the ends more than justifies the means, for if we 'but knew the glorious goal that lies beyond forgiveness' (T-29.V.6:1), our trust would be complete and our dedication strong.

6

Wholeness and Attention

There is a well-known saying in writing circles: *'Kill your darlings!'*. The phrase is advice from American writer William Faulkner, winner of the Nobel Prize for literature in 1949. Faulkner meant that we need to let go of the bits of our writing we love but that, in the cold light of reason, we know don't really fit. We hold on to those precious bits (here I picture Tolkien's *Gollum* with the ring) because we think they are something special, impressive, *awesome* even.

Writing a book takes a lot of work. For most, it involves a great deal of research and time spent going down several avenues only to later discard much of what you've gathered or written. That's normal. After recently publishing my own book, however, I wondered how much time I'd spent focussing on things that had become 'special' to me, only to discard them later because they didn't further the book's main message or purpose. Could I be more efficient in the future? Was I in a different mindset when going off track, to when I wasn't?

It didn't take much reflection to realise that going off on a 'special' tangent did indeed involve a particular way of approaching my work. Firstly, I'd get excited about a new avenue I'd discovered. Excitement was quickly followed by obsessiveness and compulsively jumping from one new source of information to another, until my thought processes became very, very *complex*. Whilst energised by the thought of the connections I was making, I also became super focussed, absorbed in the task at hand, and.... niggly. I didn't like being distracted. Indeed, my mind was in a constant battle with anything, and anyone, who might take me away from my *precious* task.

That was on what I'd call, in hindsight, a 'bad day'. On a *good* day, things were quite different. I was far more relaxed. I didn't mind being disturbed and I didn't feel any sense of urgency. In essence, my mind was a lot quieter. I still mightn't have later included all the information I acquired during these times, but it certainly shaped the end result, and in many cases has been useful to me for other reasons.

Reflecting on these two mindsets I was reminded of J. Krishnamurti's distinction between concentration and attention. Concentration, said Krishnamurti, is like interest — the interest of a child playing with a toy for example. Such concentrated interest fully absorbs the child's mind and can be very pleasing, but as soon as the toy is taken away, the child becomes restless. Likewise, adults can become restless if they can't champion a cause, don't have a DIY project, or otherwise can't become *lost* in something. In such cases, concentration is a distraction from discomfort. It's also a distraction from *attending to the mind*.

That's what Krishnamurti defines as attention — a state in which we maintain an awareness of our mind — of where it's at — and an openness that is receptive. Attention has a much wider scope than concentration. There is also a lack of drivenness with attention: there is no compulsion to act based on fear or trying to become or create something great, and so the mind is relatively still and spacious, allowing us to *listen*.

To attend, then, is to identify with the wholeness, safety and magnitude of our Self. In contrast, when we are striving, focussed on gaining or becoming, we have (to paraphrase the Course) 'contented ourselves with littleness' (T-15.III.1:1), and it won't be long before our overzealous enthusiasm turns to frustration and confusion, because a mind identified with the ego will always be in conflict, leading to inefficiency.

From Time to Timelessness

The act of listening, of truly attending, is an end in itself because it affirms the reality of our wholeness: if we're listening, we have 'arrived'. There is nothing to strive for, we 'need do nothing' (T-18.VII), and so there is no need for time. The quality of what we do 'do' from this space will be very different to when we're trying to achieve something for the future or make something happen.

I saw a documentary once about a group of budding pianists attending a piano masterclass, and a moment between the instructor and one of the students beautifully illustrated this point. The student — a man in his early twenties — was playing a piece for the instructor, and although he hit all the right notes there was something a bit 'off' about his performance.

After a few attempts by the instructor to convey what she felt was missing, she sat at the piano herself and began to play. 'See', she said, *'there is no time'*. It was a wonderful way of describing the difference between the quality of her playing and that of the student's. The instructor wasn't playing to arrive anywhere, to *do*, *achieve*, or *gain* anything. She was playing from a place where she had already arrived. That place will also be a place of love, because it doesn't ask for anything.

Attention therefore is a state in which we feel a sense of rest, no matter how busy we appear to be. But how do we achieve it? How do we identify with timelessness? In the Course, the 'Holy Instant' is a moment in which we choose to step out of the chain of time — to stop striving to gain or avoid something (always based on shame and guilt and oriented to the future to escape the past). The Holy Instant is a moment in the 'Now', but it's not necessarily experienced by trying to bring yourself into the present moment, though that can be relaxing and helpful at times.

The Course's 'Now' refers to a timeless state that doesn't know of 'past' or 'future', and is a by-product of forgiveness — of letting go of the shame and guilt behind our judgements, compulsions and striving. We don't try to be in the Now — or to 'concentrate' on the present moment — but to remove the obstructions to experiencing it. The following extract from the Course referring to the timeless magnitude of our Self and the timebound littleness of the ego self also emphasises the Course's path of undoing the negative to experience the positive:

You don't have to strive for it [magnitude], because you have it. All your striving must be directed against littleness, for it does require vigilance to protect your magnitude in this world (T-15.III.4:3-4).

We can replace the word 'magnitude' in the above quote, with 'the Now', love, peace or freedom. Our task isn't to seek for these things directly, but to be vigilant for when we identify with the ego's littleness. So, we notice when we're feeling a bit agitated, or our mind's busy, or we've become so absorbed in a task that we don't want to stop and get that glass of water we should have got half an hour ago. Our thinking is likely to have been more confused, intense, and our attempts at problem-solving unprofitable.

In our restlessness there is no quietness, no listening, no inspiration, only endless perspiration. That's when we stop, pan out, and observe what we're doing. We've identified with littleness, with shame and guilt, and have let them lead the way. It's simply in observing what we're doing and being aware of the choice we have made that we're able to make a different choice. The truth of who we are will have its own action as we ask for Help (from whatever symbol represents Higher

Guidance) to look at our decision for the ego with us. We might then feel inspired to take a break, listen to some music, or carry on but from a larger perspective.

The challenge to 'attending', however, doesn't end with over-zealous concentration. There is an equally problematic agent in the mix: *procrastination*. Concentration and procrastination are two sides of the 'distraction' coin when it comes to attention. Just as 'kill your darlings' is a well-known saying amongst writers, so too is the fact that housework never seems so appealing as when there's writing to be done. When you're stuck in compulsive concentration mode, you can't wrench yourself away from work, and when you're in procrastination mode, you can't even countenance the thought of doing it. Procrastination can be another form of resistance to joining with our Self, particularly if we've become mindful of how valuable a particular activity has become as a way of experiencing such joining.

I think the Course provides helpful advice for those times when you're not sure whether to 'lean in' and sit yourself (and your procrastination) down at your desk, or to let yourself take a breather and do anything and everything *but* write. Regarding doing the Course's workbook lessons, we're told if we feel some resistance when we sit quietly with eyes closed, to wait a few moments to see if the resistance lessens. If it doesn't, that's fine, we should let ourselves open our eyes and do what we feel to do. Likewise, if we dip our toes into the task that we've been avoiding, we might find that we become interested and happy to continue with it, or that we feel worse or even resentful – then we should stop and let ourselves off the hook.

All this talk of concentration, procrastination, and attention isn't just relevant to writers, or to any kind of work. It's relevant for every moment of the day, every circumstance, and every decision we face. How do we approach what's before us? Do we assume we're on our own, that it's all up to us, that our livelihood, safety and happiness depends on our own intellect, body, or talent? If we do, our awareness will narrow down, and we'll be in a concentrated, problem-solving mindset. That's heavy-going, and ultimately lonely.

When we find ourselves concentrating hard on the conversation we just had, on whether or not we/they said the right thing, or on what to have for dinner, or what we're planning to do tomorrow, we have narrowed our awareness down to ourselves, alone in the world with the weight of every decision and possibility on our shoulders. To the ego, this is great and satisfying because the ego itself 'is the mind's belief that it is completely on its own' (T-4.II.8:4). But we will tire of it eventually — the constant judging, planning, and second-guessing.

In the end, what really helps us to 'attend', is to trust that we're not alone, that there is a source of support and love that is open to us for inspiration and comfort, giving us 'rest in the midst of every busy doing on which [we] are sent' (T-18.VII.8:3.). Then whatever we do will have a sense of 'poetry' about it. As Plato said: 'At the touch of love, everyone becomes a poet'.

7

Outrageous Requests

One of the most important distinctions *A Course in Miracles* makes is between form and content — between what someone says or does for example (form), and the ultimate motivation for their actions (content). Without being mindful of this distinction, we can easily misinterpret sections of the Course as giving a prescription for behaviour. A commonly misunderstood passage occurs in chapter twelve, and refers to the 'outrageous requests' of others:

Recognize what does not matter, and if your brothers ask you for something 'outrageous,' do it because it does not matter (T-12.III.4).

I heard of a woman interpreting this passage to mean that she should start wearing makeup because her boyfriend asked her to. Cue the familiar parental refrain: *'and if they asked you to jump off a bridge, would you do that too?!'*.

The Course clarifies the above passage, four chapters later, with the following:

I have said that if a brother asks a foolish thing of you to do it. But be certain

that this does not mean to do a foolish thing that would hurt either him or
you, for what would hurt one will hurt the other (T-16.I.6:4-5).

While this passage seems to clarify the first, it can further muddy
the waters if not interpreted within the Course's broader context and
message. What exactly does the above passage mean by 'hurt'? Does it
mean to be damaged physically? If so, then the 'harmless' act of putting
on makeup at someone's request, for example, can seem like the thing to
do. But what about other, non-physical, ramifications? What about the
notion of being authentic? If we do something that we really don't want
to do, won't we resent it? And won't resentment (suppressed anger)
eventually come out sideways as anxiety? (Yes, it will.)

The Course's message can only be interpreted helpfully by remembering it is always talking about what goes on in our mind; specifically,
the judgements we make about others and ourselves. In other words,
the Course is concerned with the *meaning* we attribute to things.

Meaning-Makers

We are constantly telling ourselves stories about what things mean: why
people do what they do, and why we react in a particular way. If we see
someone trip on a rug, for example, we might think they are clumsy, or
alternatively that the rug is the problem — perhaps there is a loose thread
or the rug is too thick, thereby posing a hazard. (Nine times out of ten,
however, we will attribute the cause of misfortune to a characteristic of
the sufferer, something psychologists call the Fundamental Attribution
Error. When we are identified with our ego, we are indeed primed to
judge others harshly.)

The fact that we are meaning-makers — and that our inner experience
is inextricably linked to the meanings or interpretations we generate
— is why the first lessons in the Course focus on helping us loosen our

grip on our habitual perceptions. The lessons bring home the fact that we have given everything we see a meaning, and these meanings will be based on lessons from our past. We don't, therefore, see anything as it truly is now, because our interpretations are based on past-associations, clouding our vision. How many times, for example, has someone totally misunderstood what you've said, becoming offended (or flattered) when this wasn't intended. In such cases, our actions may have been misconstrued according to that person's past experience: they heard, or saw, what they expected.

Referring back to the issue of 'outrageous requests', what the Course is asking us to consider is that the meaning behind such a request isn't what it appears to be. In other words, based on the *form* of someone's request, it seems that they are asking us to do something in particular, and that their happiness depends on us doing what they ask on this level, the level of form. But on the level of the mind — the level of *content* — they are asking for something quite different, something they themselves are unaware of.

The more a person presses us to do something, the more they believe their salvation lies in us doing it. At that point, they have identified with their ego and the sense of lack, deprivation and insecurity that go with such identification. To identify with the ego is to believe we have separated from God, Love and Wholeness. The sense of anxiety and depression that stems from this has us turning to the world for comfort, rather than to our minds where the source of the problem lies:

To identify with the ego is to attack yourself and make yourself poor. That is why everyone who identifies with the ego feels deprived... He does not realise this. Even if he is fully aware of anxiety he does not perceive the source as his own ego identification, and he always tries to handle it by making some sort of insane 'arrangement' with the world (T-12.III.6:1-5).

We get an idea that doing or having A, B, or C will make us feel better, and in the hope of easing our distress, we become heavily invested in getting what we want, even if this means getting someone else to do what they don't want to do. When someone gets what they want on the level of form, however, this doesn't answer their real request — to be shown that they haven't separated from love, though they believe they have thrown it away. It is the peace in our mind that remains undisturbed by their choice for the ego and their 'outrageous' request, that mirrors back to them the peace and love that remains in their mind, and this is the real source of help.

According to the Course, there are ultimately two motivations underlying all behaviour: to call for love/help, or to express love. As our peace and lack of judgement answers someone's call for help, it reminds them that there is another choice they can make. From this peaceful place, we are able to listen to the guidance of the Holy Spirit and do whatever we feel to do on the level of form. We can say 'no' on the level of form as long as we have answered someone's true request by not judging them. That's the ideal, but what if we *do* find ourselves reacting strongly to the requests of others?

Our Sole Responsibility

Ideally, we don't answer someone's request on the level of form until we have answered it on the level of content, and we can't do this while we are judging them and ourselves. If we feel an intense reaction to someone's request, then we first need to attend to our mind, becoming aware of anything that would cause us to feel at odds with (and therefore separate from) them. Feelings of being impinged upon, let-down, unconsidered, harassed, along with disgust, fear or anger are red flags that there's something for us to look at. We can't answer someone's call for help until will have looked at the judgements which have elicited these emotions, and choose to have them corrected, or 'judge against' them:

You cannot lay aside the obstacles to real vision without looking upon them, for to lay aside means to judge against (T-12.II.9:6).

By looking at our own judgements and choice for the ego, we are able to first forgive ourselves before we forgive someone else, no longer judging them for their own misguided choice:

The sole responsibility of the miracle worker is to accept the Atonement for himself... Once you accept this, your mind can only heal (T-2.V.5:1).

If what someone wants us to do seems to cause us to lose our peace, then it symbolises something to us – something that needs forgiving. In the makeup situation for example, if the woman was to respond with indignation (*'How dare you?!'*), then she could ask herself if she would condemn herself for such a request. Perhaps, for example, she'd harboured a wish that her boyfriend act in a more (or less) refined way, or dressed differently, or had a better, more impressive job, or lost (or gained) some weight (none of these for his sake, but for her own satisfaction). She might never have verbalised her wishes, but, like him, she had felt that her happiness depended on her partner being different.

Having noticed this, she could ask the Holy Spirit for help to forgive herself for having identified with the ego in the past and present. Alternatively, if she had reacted to the request with depression and emotional withdrawal rather than indignation, chances are she was interpreting things through the lens of the past — of never feeling good enough. The temptation for her then might be to go ahead and wear makeup, but do it with a sense of resignation, having interpreted her boyfriend's request as yet another confirmation of her inherent unworthiness.

If, however, she manages to notice her emotional reaction to the request, and looks at it with the Holy Spirit who reminds her of her inherent worthiness, she has the opportunity to use the situation to forgive those in the past she blames for her lack of self-worth, along with her partner for the meaning she'd perceived in his request. In doing this she'd fulfill her one responsibility — to see the situation through the eyes of forgiveness, rather than judgement. Whatever she did or didn't do from this point on would be secondary, and wouldn't involve the inner conflict she'd otherwise have felt regardless of what she chose to do in form.

In asking for help to see things differently, we create space in our mind to let the Holy Spirit show us the way forward. Then whatever we feel to do won't be a big deal for us, and it will be in the form through which we both can accept the message of forgiveness and the joining between us, realising that we are both being healed and therefore *both gaining*. Such joining can happen whether we do the 'outrageous' thing or not. This is what's so hard to grasp when we are focussed on the world of form, and is another example of how the Course's curriculum represents a thought system that is totally opposite to what we are accustomed to.

So, when the Course says, 'Recognise what does not matter, and if your brothers ask you for something "outrageous", do it because it does not matter' (T-12.III.4), it is saying *look beyond the form of the request, because the form doesn't matter*. But the only way we can look beyond the form and answer the call for help behind it is to first notice our judgements. Then we can answer the true request by letting the Holy Spirit remind us both of who we are. As the Course says, we are never healed alone (W-130.10:3).

8

The Authority Problem

We all have to assume authority to lesser and greater degrees throughout life. If you've ever had to give your opinion about something or make a decision (and who hasn't done *that*?!), you've had to step — if only for a moment — into a position of authority. Having authority means having power to direct your own course and perhaps those of others. The opposite of having authority is being helpless and dependent — something we are all familiar with from childhood.

Some people are happy to be in a position of authority; others shrink from it. What if we (or others) follow our direction and things go wrong? The sense of responsibility can be overwhelming. On the other hand, some people revel in the idea of having authority and have no problem telling people what to do. Assuming a position of authority, however, doesn't necessarily mean we have accepted the responsibilities that go with it: often people in powerful positions disregard how their choices affect others and readily pass the buck when things go wrong.

These two extreme ways of relating to personal authority develop largely in response to our relationships with the primary authority figures in our early childhood — typically our parents — and influence every facet of our adult lives. However, according to *A Course in Miracles*, the way we experience our worldly relationships reflects our imagined relationship to God.

An Unloving Parent

There are two things we want most from our parents. To feel valued (recognised as something special) and the freedom to be who we are (an individual distinct from our parents) without the threat of abandonment or punishment. This reflects the ontological 'parent-child' situation between ourselves and God: in the Course's myth of the world's origins, we were at peace as a part of God's undifferentiated oneness until we wanted God to notice us as something special, something different from everything else. God, however, *couldn't* see us as something special because that would require us to be separate and different — an impossibility within an abstract, undifferentiated unity. Personally affronted by God's seeming snub, we 'made of Him an unloving father', one who didn't give us the attention we craved because he didn't love us.

Not only did we want to be special, we wanted to be independent and autonomous; we wanted to assert ourselves, and be free of God's creative authority. This wish to extricate ourselves from our dependence on God made us feel guilty and fearful of God's retribution.

According to the Course, all fear, can be traced back to these two elements regarding our original 'authority problem' with God: 1) Turning our back on God's love and oneness, we fear retribution or disaster for any 'authoritative' move we make in the world; 2) feeling overlooked and insignificant — nothing 'special' — we are sensitive to people dismissing us, and fear abandonment. We project the imagined conflict between ourselves and God out of our mind and perceive a world in which we fear retaliation and abandonment, and ourselves attack and reject others.

A *Course in Miracles* addresses this belief and shows how our unconscious authority problem between ourselves and God is at the root of all our distress:

I have spoken of different symptoms, and at that level there is almost endless variation. There is, however, only one cause for all of them: the authority problem (T-3.VI.7:1-3).

Of all the many causes you perceived as bringing pain and suffering to you, your guilt was not among them (T-27.VII.7:4).

Guilt feelings... induce fears of retaliation or abandonment... (T-5.VI.2:1-2).

While the Course refers to guilt as our main problem, it's important to note that the Course uses the word 'guilt' to encapsulate other 'negative' feelings such as inferiority, which are generally associated with shame. The distinction is important because whether we identify more from shame or with guilt will influence the way we relate to our own authority, reflecting one of two distinct responses to the 'authority problem'.

Shame, Guilt and the Authority Problem

My book, *Above the Battleground: The Courageous Path to Emotional Autonomy and Inner Peace,* provides an in-depth discussion of shame and guilt, and provides the background research for the following (brief) discussion.

Essentially, shame relates to feeling overlooked, discarded and inferior, and its associated fear is of abandonment, while guilt relates to having broken a moral code or law and its associated fear is of retribution. In relation to our parents, if we feel they attend to (value) something else more than ourselves we'll feel inferior, experience shame, and fear abandonment. If we suspect that our attempts at independence (embodying our own sense of self and personal power) displeases our parents, we'll feel guilt and fear retribution.

Returning to the discussion at the beginning of this post, people who suffer more shame-anxiety than guilt-anxiety tend to be the ones who revel in the idea of having power. Their need to make up for painful feelings of inferiority, however, make them prone to acting irresponsibility within their role. The biggest fear isn't that they might hurt someone, but of being helpless or considered weak. In contrast, people prone to more guilt-anxiety tend to shy away from the idea of power and authority, and feel overly responsible for the welfare of others.

How then, do we approach the prospect of having authority without fearing we'll cause disaster, nor with the idea that it removes us from accountability? How do we become a 'good' authority — one who is both sensitive to the needs of others, and able to make decisions and put their ideas into action?

How to be a Good Authority: Retracing Our Steps

If all our distress stems from a belief that we offended God (guilt) and that He overlooked us (shame), healing then becomes a matter of knowing that *nothing happened*. As part of an undifferentiated unity, we couldn't possibly even *conceive* of being apart from our source; nor could we wish to be noticed as something special. It's as if a part of oneness fell asleep and dreamed a dream in which it could actually think apart from God.

Fortunately, the way we release our identification with shame and guilt doesn't involve focusing on the somewhat brain-bending aspects of the Course's metaphysics (*'How could the impossible happen?'*). Instead, the focus is on addressing the shame and guilt we feel in relationships — particularly with the major authority figures in our lives. In this way, we work indirectly with our unconscious relationship to God. It's also how we slowly grow into an experience that affirms the message of the Course's metaphysics: that we are inherently worthy. Our ego self mightn't be innocent (guilt), and may sometimes be the subject of scorn (shame), but we are not our ego self.

It's in looking at how we perceive our relationships and the world that we gain access to what we secretly believe about ourselves, God, and our relationship to Him. With the Holy Spirit's help, we retrace our steps from our authority problems in the world, back to the authority problem within the mind. We look at the specific instances of feeling rejected or punished, our hatreds and our grief, and ask for help to see things differently. The Holy Spirit gives us a perspective from 'above the battleground', a perspective that knows of our innocence and wholeness, and of God's eternal love.

To be a good authority, therefore, we need to address the authority problems with our parents which are projected out onto other authority figures in our lives. The attention we never got from a parent, for example, we might seek from various medical professionals, or our boss, partner, or sporting coach. We begin to depend on others to meet our emotional needs, to feel valued and approved of, and we feel dejected or furious if these needs aren't met. How can we be a good authority ourselves when we are so emotionally dependent? The importance of liberating ourselves from the needs of the past is highlighted in the following passage from Freud's paper 'Family Romances':

The freeing of an individual, as he grows up, from the authority of his parents is one of the most necessary though one of the most painful results brought about by the course of his development. It is quite essential that that liberation should occur and it may be presumed that it has been to some extent achieved by everyone who has reached a normal state.

Many people misunderstand Freud to mean that unless a child has moved out of home, for example, they have not moved on from the authority of their parents. This is, to use a Course phrase, to mistake form for content. Freud is talking about the child's inner experience of who they are as a distinct being apart from their parents, and of their gradual realisation that their parents aren't gods and aren't always right. Whether they happen to be at home following household rules or living in their own place, free to do as they please, is beside the point. We free ourselves from the authority of our parents by realising that neither they nor our many parental substitutes have the authority to dictate our worth.

As children, we gave our parents (and society at large) that authority, hence our shame and guilt, but as adults we can choose to free ourselves from the authority of their misperceptions. By no longer using the misperceptions of others as the basis for our self-image, we lose our emotional neediness and the drive to appear better, stronger, more powerful, or good. We now realise (through the process of forgiveness) that *we* are the one who is limiting our freedom, and *we* are the one who is devaluing us by continuing to believe a lie.

As we apply the process of forgiveness to all circumstances in which we feel belittled, undervalued, and small, for example, we realise that our sense of self-worth is a matter for ourselves alone — that we can stand tall regardless of circumstances because of who we really are. In so doing we would also be accepting our equality with those who seemed to attack us, because we are accepting the truth that we are *all* 'special'.

Every educator knows that it is difficult for people to learn something when they are in a fearful or agitated state. The thought-processes become jumbled and the simplest of tasks can appear taxing. To be able to learn from our inner Teacher and follow their guidance reliably, we need to be free of the anxieties of shame and guilt. Through the process of forgiveness we become better acquainted with 'the stately calm within'(T-18.I.8:2), thus enabling us to let the loving inner Authority teach and work through us. Somewhat ironically, it's in realising our dependence on the inner Authority to help us forgive, that we are freed of our emotional dependence on others, a prerequisite for being a good authority.

9

The Last Refuge

In Season Two, episode fourteen of *The Simpsons*, Bart faces one of his biggest fears. No stranger to failing exams, Bart is warned that he will have to repeat the fourth grade if he fails an upcoming history exam. Terrified of this eventuality, he enlists the help of Martin, the class overachiever, in exchange for teaching Martin how to be cool. Bart's bargain backfires however as Martin becomes intoxicated with his new popularity. Left to study on his own and woefully ill-prepared for the next day's test, Bart prays to God, begging for a snow storm to close the school. Bart's sister Lisa observes him and reflects, 'Prayer; the last refuge of a scoundrel'.

And so it is with all of us, 'scoundrel' or not. There are certain, special, issues that we insist on dealing with ourselves, neglecting to address them through the process of forgiveness because they are so deeply wedded to our self-concept and experience of the world: to let go of them would be to be 'reborn' in a profound way. We in fact seek refuge *in these issues and our habitual ways of dealing with them*, because they have become a potent means of maintaining our ego-identification and sense of separation from God.

Special Relationships

In the Course's myth, once we believed that we had separated from God and made a self apart from His oneness, we then experienced ourselves as incomplete and deprived. We also became fearful of retribution for our perceived attack on God, having turned our back on His love and attacked His authority. What, then, do we turn to in order to feel better; to fill the hole and mask our fear?

The Course uses the term 'special relationships' for those relationships we cling to as a substitute for our relationship with God. A 'special love' relationship is one in which we seek to get something to fill our sense of lack and deficiency. We can have a special love relationship with a job that gives us status or a sense of self-worth for example, or with a person who we believe completes us in some way, or gives us the love and attention we secretly believe we don't deserve.

When we don't get what we want from our special love objects, special love turns to hate. Hate is also a means of masking our fear: by saying someone else is the cause of our misery, we are able to displace our guilt for having chosen the ego in the first place.

Whatever we turn to instead of appealing to our right mind to feel better is an object of specialness. Addictions of any kind are special relationships. We can love the relief a drug (for example) seems to give us from painful feelings, but hate our dependency on it and its other detrimental effects on our life. We can also be addicted to money, whether we have a lot of it or not: we look to it to feel secure, or blame all of our suffering on never having enough. We might not be addicted physiologically to money, but issues surrounding it can cause us the deepest distress: we feel good when we have it, down when we don't, and it can consume our attention as much as any drug.

A special relationship, then, is the result of a conclusion that we are incomplete and need to provide for our own safety because we are essentially alone. Indeed, the ego is the embodiment of the thought that we are alone, no longer supported by God's oneness, and our special relationships reflect our substitutes for our dependency on Him.

The Appointed Friend

In this world, an acceptance of our dependence on God is reflected by an acceptance that *forgiveness* 'offers us everything we want' (W.141). But, we become so preoccupied with managing our special relationships ourselves that we forget to seek refuge in forgiveness and the perspective of the Holy Spirit, our 'appointed Friend':

Every special relationship you have made has, as its fundamental purpose, the aim of occupying your mind so completely that you will not hear the call of truth (T- 17.IV.3:3).

Who dwells with shadows is alone indeed, and loneliness is not the Will of God... Make no illusion friend, for if you do, it can but take the place of Him Whom God has called your Friend (T-26.VI.3:1, 3).

Eventually, however, the pain associated with even the special relationship we cling to the most is enough to make us pause in despair, finally acknowledging that there must be a better way of approaching things:

Tolerance for pain may be high, but it is not without limit. Eventually everyone begins to recognize, however dimly, that there must be a better way. As this recognition becomes more firmly established, it becomes a turning point. This ultimately reawakens spiritual vision, simultaneously weakening the investment in physical sight (T-2.III.3:5-8).

The recognition that there must be a better way 'reawakens spiritual vision' because it suggests that there must be another, 'more enlightened', way of looking at the situation at hand:

Belief that there is another way of perceiving is the loftiest idea of which ego thinking is capable. That is because it contains a hint of recognition that the ego is not the Self (T-4.II.4:10-11).

Once we allow the situation to be used for the purpose of forgiveness and letting go of our ego, we can feel a lightness of spirit, followed not long after by our usual response (anger, fear, resentment). This is because, at least initially, we will still be in two minds about how we want to look at the relationship — through the lens of our ego (which will perceive victims and victimisers, winners and losers, the worthy and unworthy), or with the vision of the Holy Spirit (which sees no blame, nor cause for distress):

The alternating investment in the two levels of perception is usually experienced as conflict, which can become very acute (T-2.III.3:9).

But we are assured that this time will pass; that 'the outcome is as certain as God' (T-2.III.3:10).

The Road to Damascus Moment

Prayer, or asking for help to see things from the perspective of Truth, marks the beginning of the end of our ego, and this is why it is our last refuge when it comes to our most special relationships. Where the hidden purpose of our special relationship was to drown out the voice of the Holy Spirit, we now use it as a means of establishing communication with it. Our special relationship becomes holy as we use it to turn within and develop reliance and trust on the voice for God. Giving up our addiction therefore symbolises giving up the ego.

This is why Carl Jung suggested that the path to full recovery from alcoholism would most likely involve a 'conversion' experience. Bill Wilson, the founder of Alcoholics Anonymous in 1934, was influenced by Jung's experience with a patient called Mr. Rowland, an investment banker, former senator from Rhode Island, and an alcoholic. Rowland improved after seeing Jung for therapy, however after a relapse, Jung suggested that real hope lay only in a 'religious conversion'.

Jung used religious language metaphorically. By 'religious conversion' he didn't mean for Rolland to join a religion. He was suggesting that he avail himself of his spiritual nature, give credence to it, or make room for it. This, for example, was how he interpreted Saint Paul's conversion to Christianity whilst travelling along the road to Damascus. Jung viewed Paul's vision of Jesus as a projection of his own spirituality calling to him for integration.

The problem with many addictions, or special relationships, is that people give them up on the level of form without addressing the 'spiritual thirst' (as Jung put it) that underpins them. It's not uncommon then for people to return to the addictive behaviour or develop another addiction, or for their romantic relationship to once again become filled with conflict. The spiritual thirst, in Course terms, would be to know of our innocent, spiritual Self. In looking at any special relationship, therefore, we really want to give up our dependence on the ego's judgements. We do this by seeking refuge in forgiveness, asking the Holy Spirit's help to release those from our past whom we hold responsible for developing our addictions.

Healing also involves asking for help to look at and forgive our choice for the ego. It would be helpful, for example, to look at how we have conducted ourselves in regard to our special relationship. Have we habitually tried to 'do people over' in business transactions for example, in order to meet a need to feel triumphant, or to keep a tight hold on our money even though we have 'enough'?

The point of looking isn't to feel guilty, but to highlight how our *investment* in getting certain things is linked to a 'one-or-the-other' mindset in which someone else must lose in order for us to get what we want. This creates a vicious cycle in which guilt over having chosen to identify with our ego is reinforced by our decision to see our interests as separate from someone else's. With the Holy Spirit's help, we will understand that our attitude stemmed from fear, and that fear calls for love, not punishment. The ego, in contrast, would never let us off the hook, because it feeds on making mistakes into BIG DEALS.

As our faith moves from our special relationships, past our belief in separation 'and on to reason' (T-21.IV.4.3), we are met with the reality of our Self, and this heralds the end of our ego. We are assured in the Course's psychotherapy pamphlet that if we need something (such as money) to help us 'better serve the plan' (our path of forgiveness), then it will be given to us (P-3.III.1:4). And as we continue to seek refuge in the process of forgiveness, we will experience a sense of true happiness and peace that we know isn't contingent on anything external. All we need do is decide that we 'will accept God's peace and joy, in glad exchange for all the substitutes that [we] have made for happiness and peace (W.118)'.

10

Cleaning the Mirror

A *Course in Miracles* is as a course in recognition: firstly, we learn to recognise the kind of thoughts that are part of the ego thought system; then we are taught how to let go of them through forgiveness, enabling us to recognise our Self — our true identity — and this brings us peace. Recognition of what hurts us, followed by its removal — that's the Course's recipe for healing:

What is healing but the removal of all that stands in the way of knowledge [love, the Self]? And how else can one dispel illusions except by looking at them directly, without protecting them? (T-11.V.2:1-2).

So, while the Course leads us towards love, it's curriculum focusses on helping us recognise all that is *not* love: 'That is the interference; that is what needs to be undone' (T-18.IX.12:4).

What Love is Not

The Course says there are two emotions or, rather, two motivations for all of our actions: love and fear. It also says that 'frightened people can be vicious' (T-3.I.4:2). Fear breeds attack, yet the forms attack can take aren't always obvious; some even come with a smile and the best of intentions. Indeed, the Course makes it clear that we don't realise all the forms in which we attack others and ourselves:

Is it not true you do not recognize some of the forms attack can take? If it is true attack in any form will hurt you, and will do so just as much as in another form that you do recognize, then it must follow that you do not always recognize the source of pain. Attack in any form is equally destructive (T-23.III.1:1-3).

Attacking others will hurt us because it will feed our guilt. So, while we can't always recognise when we are attacking, we can at least recognise the signs:

There is a stab of pain, a twinge of guilt, and above all, a loss of peace (T-23.IV.6:3).

A lack of peace is therefore one sign that we have chosen to attack, and choosing to value *any aspect* of the ego thought system is itself an attack on love, 'an assault on truth' (T-23.IV.1:12), and we'll feel guilty and agitated because of it.

Workbook lesson 133, 'I will not value what is valueless', provides a guide for distinguishing between what is valueless (anything the ego holds dear) and what is valuable (anything that reinforces our true identity):

Today we list the real criteria by which to test all things you think you want. Unless they meet these sound requirements, they are not worth desiring at all, for they can but replace what offers more... it is wise to learn the laws you set in motion when you choose, and what alternatives you choose between (W-133.3:1-2, 5).

If we don't realise how to distinguish between what is valuable and valueless, we won't know when we are choosing sorrow over happiness, or attack over love, and these are the only alternatives we ever choose between:

We have already stressed there are but two [alternatives], however many there appear to be... Each choice you make brings everything to you or nothing. Therefore, if you learn the tests by which you can distinguish everything from nothing, you will make the better choice (W-133.4:1; 5:3-4).

All that Glitters: Distinguishing the Valuable from the Valueless

The workbook lesson gives four criteria for what is valuable:

1. It must be eternal.

Basically, anything outside of ourselves (including our own body) doesn't last. The world is a place of change where people and things come and go, and as the Stoic philosopher Seneca said, 'fortune gives us nothing we can truly own'. To seek for something outside of yourself as the be-all-and-end-all, the answer to all your problems, is to set yourself up for pain:

Seek not outside yourself. For it will fail, and you will weep each time an

51

idol falls... For all your pain comes simply from a futile search for what you want, insisting where it must be found... No one who comes here but must still have hope, some lingering illusion, or some dream that there is something outside of himself that will bring happiness and peace to him. If everything is in him this cannot be so... Seek not outside yourself. The search implies you are not whole within and fear to look upon your devastation, but prefer to seek outside yourself for what you are (T-29.VII.1:1-2, 7; 2:1-2; 4:5-6).

In contrast, our Self shares the timelessness of Heaven, and the daily practice of forgiveness is how we come to identify with its wholeness, something that the ego tries to prevent by insisting that happiness can be found outside, in something we can consume or possess:

All idols of this world were made to keep the truth within from being known to you, and to maintain allegiance to the dream that you must find what is outside yourself to be complete and happy (T-29.VII.6:1).

The ego is all about 'getting', whereas our right-minded Self simply 'is'. The problem is we don't know the difference between pain and joy. We think joy is having our specialness needs filled — in feeling superior to others, for example, or desirable, or vindicated. Having our emotional needs filled feels great for a moment, but it creates a dependency, and one that can't be counted on. Does fame or status last for ever? Do you have it everywhere and with everyone? Can it be lost? What is it vulnerable to? What about your looks or health?

The Course isn't suggesting that we should deny ourselves worldly things that appeal to us, but that worldly things, in and of themselves, won't make us happy, and to believe that they can is to identify with littleness:

You do not ask too much of life, but far too little. When you let your mind be drawn to bodily concerns, to things you buy, to eminence as valued by the world, you ask for sorrow, not for happiness. This course does not attempt to take from you the little that you have (W-133.2:1-3).

When you choose for things of the world *above all else*, we cut ourselves off from what we already have, the only gift that can satisfy; a gift we recognise through practicing forgiveness:

What could you want forgiveness cannot give? Do you want peace? Forgiveness offers it. Do you want happiness, a quiet mind, a certainty of purpose, and a sense of worth and beauty that transcends the world? Do you want care and safety, and the warmth of sure protection always? Do you want a quietness that cannot be disturbed, a gentleness that never can be hurt, a deep abiding comfort, and a rest so perfect it can never be upset? (W-122.1:1-6).

We are assured that forgiveness offers us all of this. The problem is, we don't yet believe that a quiet mind and transcendent sense of worth and beauty will satisfy us more than getting a new car, bigger house, an award, or more followers on [insert your preferred social media platform]:

Obey the Holy Spirit, and you will be giving up the ego. But you will be sacrificing nothing. On the contrary, you will be gaining everything. If you believed this, there would be no conflict (T-7.X.3:8-11).

2. It must be something that is shared.

The ego thought system (founded on a belief in separation) is all about separate interests, one-or-the-other, winners and losers. The ego thrives on making comparisons — who has more, who has less — and comparisons ultimately lead to judgements of better and worse, inferior and superior. Sameness is the enemy of the ego. In fact, the ego has no concept of it:

It [the world's perception] rests on differences; on uneven background and shifting foreground, on unequal heights and diverse sizes, on varying degrees of darkness and light, and thousands of contrasts in which each thing seen competes with every other in order to be recognized. A larger object overshadows a smaller one. A brighter thing draws the attention from another with less intensity of appeal... What the body's eyes behold is only conflict. Look not to them for peace and understanding.... Illusions are always illusions of differences (M-8.1:2-4, 6-7; 2:1).

Through the body's eyes we see a world of differences, and these differences *mean something important* to us. Through the Holy Spirit's vision, we are able to recognise the sameness (we share the same fears, and same need to return Home) beyond the differences in form, and *that* is what matters most; that is what we value. This is how we shift from identifying with the body to the Self that is beyond it: we recognise our sameness. We are all worthy, we are all perfect. Not some of us, but *all* of us.

A helpful exercise is to go about your day noticing all of the ways in which you habitually emphasise and judge differences, making them into a big deal. If we believe we have something *special* that someone else doesn't — knowledge, money, status, an education — we have again placed value on the valueless. In any interaction, what we give or take on the level of form (information, money, time) is secondary. What is primary is our purpose — either to focus on what I am giving you on the level of form and to therefore feel like I need something in return, or to remember our shared interests, our sameness, and in doing so answer our shared need.

The only thing that gives anything of the world value is the purpose for which it is used, and it can either be used by our right mind, or our wrong mind, for healing or attack respectively. What is valuable, then, entails no loss to anyone.

3. It doesn't serve the ego's secret goal of perpetuating our individuality or guilt.

The ego feeds on guilt and is sustained by it. It will therefore do whatever it can to get us to do or perceive something so as to increase our guilt, but never let this secret goal be obvious to us. Indeed, it will do what it can to convince us that our goal is worthy, harmless, and desirable.

A classic example is the idea that it's okay to *focus* on making money because you will be able to do all sorts of good, charitable, 'loving' things with it when you have it in excess. The ideal seems harmless enough, some would say even commendable, but at its core is the tell-tale ego refrain, 'If only'.

An 'if only' orientation ('*If only I had more money; if only he/she were kinder; If only my work was recognised; If only I could live in the south of France...* ') is a statement of dependency. It says that we can't be happy until some time in the future when A, B, or C happens, and it places our state of mind, our peace, at the mercy of outside forces, many of which are beyond our control. And it is this idea — that we can't be happy now — that binds us to our ego. When we identify with our Self, however, we will be content because our Self embodies the knowledge that we already *have* everything because we *are* everything.

So, while our worldly aspirations might excite us, they will also cause us pain because they speak to a belief in our deficiency. Pretty soon, we will find ourselves making compromises based on fears associated with our experience of lack, perhaps not being totally honest with others, for example, in order to get ahead. It's this spiral downwards in our integrity — trying to gain at someone else's expense — that reveals the ego's secret goal to increase our guilt. It's also this secret goal of guilt that makes us value what can't be shared, and what isn't eternal.

4. Finally, if there is any guilt about what we have chosen (to do A or B for example), then we know we are looking at things through the ego's eyes, *regardless of whether our choice had been right-minded or not*.

Even if we had chosen with our right minds, the ego will want us to feel guilty, and have us question whether or not we had done the 'right' thing. If we had chosen with our wrong minds and can see this, it will want to rub our nose in our mistake, increasing our identification with guilt.

This focus on what we have chosen to do or not do, think or not think, keeps us in the past, obscuring 'the obvious' — that right now, if we're not feeling peaceful it's because we've chosen the ego as our interpreter. Even if we realise that we have operated from a 'one-or-the-other' mindset in the past, the Holy Spirit would never have us feel guilty. Remorse would be a more appropriate response to a mistake we made out of fear, and would enable us to move on. Reinforcing guilt, however, would ensure that we fall into the same mistake again, because it reinforces everything else about the ego thought system: fear, loneliness, deprivation, vulnerability, unworthiness and the sense of desperation that leads to a 'one-or-the-other' mentality.

In summary, *A Course in Miracles* helps us recognise the real alternatives for choice that lie before us in any circumstance, at any time. It is the choice for the valuable or valueless, happiness or sorrow, everything or nothing. Whenever there seems to be a number of choices available to us on the level of form, we're asked to notice where we are placing primary value. Do we believe our happiness depends on getting or avoiding something in particular? If so, we can be sure we are looking at the situation through the ego's eyes. But we can choose again:

You always choose between your weakness and the strength of Christ in you. And what you choose is what you think is real. Simply by never using weakness to direct your actions, you have given it no power. And the light of Christ in you is given charge of everything you do... In every difficulty, all distress, and each perplexity Christ calls to you and gently says, 'My brother, choose again' (T-31.VIII.2:3-6;3:2).

11

The Only Remaining Freedom

H anna Arendt was a German-American political philosopher who caused controversy in 1963 with the publication of *Eichmann in Jerusalem,* her report on the trial of Adolph Eichmann, an architect of the Holocaust. Arendt was struck by the apparent ordinariness of Eichmann: he didn't appear to be a 'monster', exhibit any traits distinguishing him from the everyday person in the street, or hate the victims of the 'final solution' he helped orchestrate.

Like so many other war criminals of the time (and many more since), Eichmann insisted that he had simply obeyed orders — that he wasn't, therefore, an active 'chooser' in the situations before him, but rather a person-less cog in an overarching machine.

Arendt's main point was that harm to others is sometimes done by ordinary people who 'refuse to be persons'; who refuse to see that there is any choice available to them; *who refuse to think.*

Arendt wondered if even in the most impossible of situations — where resistance to unjust or inhumane orders seems impossible — there still remains a choice: perhaps there is something between resistance and co-operation. Only *thinking,* says Arendt, will provide us with an opportunity to discover if that possibility exits. In impossible situations, thinking is our only remaining freedom.

Thinking Fresh

The kind of thinking Arendt meant wasn't our everyday, unreflective and unoriginal kind of thought that seems to have a life of its own. Arendt was greatly influenced by Socrates who responded to the Delphic Oracle's announcement that he, Socrates, was the wisest man in Athens, by saying, 'If that is so, then it's because I know that I know nothing'. For Socrates, and Arendt, the best thinking comes from letting go of all habitual judgement and perceptions, all preconceived notions of what is right or wrong, beautiful or ugly. Particularly in times of political crisis, where public rhetoric reaches fever-pitch, this kind of 'fresh' thinking is the only thing that keeps the individual from becoming a slave to the dictates of the majority; a cog in a machine. Fresh thinking therefore protects our personhood, particularly when 'the chips are down'.

In relation to *A Course in Miracles*, fresh thinking can only occur when we've chosen to listen to the Holy Spirit as our teacher, rather than the ego. This is because the ego thought system roots us in the past, whereas the Holy Spirit avails us of an ever-present, transcendent, Now. *A Course in Miracles* reminds us that no matter what goes on in the world around us, we have the power to choose with whom we want to approach the situation: the only remaining freedom lies within our mind where we can make this choice for the separating thoughts of the ego or the healing thoughts of the Holy Spirit:

In this world the only remaining freedom is the freedom of choice; always between two choices or two voices... the Holy Spirit or the ego (C-1.7:1,3).

Through the process of forgiveness, the blocks to fresh thinking are removed, and we can act in the most helpful way to all people concerned.

Challenging circumstances bring our perceptions of relationships to the fore. In every seemingly impossible situation, there can seem to be only one choice: who will win and who will lose, and in wartime this can literally be expressed as 'kill or be killed'. None of us can say how we would *behave* in extreme circumstances that highlight the 'one-or-the-other' aspect of the ego thought system, but we can help ourselves by remembering that no matter what our circumstance, we are free to bring our attention back to our mind and ask for help to look at our judgements based on differences: we will see victims and victimisers, good people and bad, oppressors and the oppressed, and we will hate and empathise accordingly.

The external problem, however, is always a mirror to our mind. Just as I see an impossible 'one-or-the-other' situation before me, I have an unconscious belief in a 'one-or-the-other' situation between myself and God; namely, that my separate existence is real and came at the cost of God's oneness. All fear comes from this belief in separation, this ontological 'one-or-the-other' situation that appears externally as 'some twisted form of the original error' (T-18.I.7:1).

My external situation now becomes an opportunity for healing as I ask for help to see beyond the separate interests of everyone involved, to our shared need — to know of our wholeness and Home. The victimisers and victims in form — perhaps sharply drawn in the circumstance before us — have this one need in common, and in recognition of this common ground we offer remembrance of oneness to all parties because we are joined at the level of mind that chooses the Holy Spirit's vision:

Therefore release him, merely by your claim on brotherhood (T-28.IV.4:3).

This is how we make room for truth. By moving beyond the temptation to hate (project our self-hatred), or to go on 'auto-pilot' to abstain from responsibility, or even to be a 'hero', we open our mind to an influence removed from the external situation yet with total knowledge of what is the most helpful response for all people concerned. This is something we could never know of ourselves, but we don't have to. Our one responsibility is to remember our only freedom and choose to make use of it. If we practice this faithfully in the seemingly small instances of 'one or the other' we encounter daily, this stands us in good stead when faced with situations that appear to present a much greater challenge.

12

The Tightrope Walker: Part One

I n a small town a crowd gathers below a tightrope spanning two towers. A hush falls over the crowd as the door of one of the towers opens and a man appears, stepping out onto the rope with a balancing pole in hand. He begins the perilous journey from one tower to the other and the crowd watches, enthralled.

As the tightrope walker nears the middle of the rope, a jester comes out of the tower behind him, taunting:

'Go on, scaredy-cat, lame-foot! Go on, lazy-bones, or I'll jump right over you! What are you doing here between the towers anyway? Go back to the tower you came from; where you should be locked up!'

The jester moves closer to the man while uttering his taunts, then jumps over him. Distraught, the tightrope walker throws away his pole and plunges to the street below.

This story is an adaptation of Friedrich Nietzsche's parable in *Thus Spoke Zarathustra*. Nietzsche saw us all as having to walk a tightrope between morality and nihilism — morality represented by the tower from which the tightrope walker emerged, and nihilism by the tower to which he was heading. Moralism refers to how we are accustomed to thinking about ethics and the meaning of life – the higher values. In every culture, we are socialised to take certain goals and expectations for granted; every culture has its ideas about what is right and wrong, worthy and unworthy. When we find through experience that the pervading culture's ideals are inadequate, we head toward the psychological state of nihilism. The philosopher Soren Kierkegaard lightheartedly expressed such disenchantment in the following:

... when I opened my eyes and saw the real world, I began to laugh and I haven't stopped since. I saw that the meaning of life was to get a livelihood, that the goal of life was to be a High Court judge, that the bright joy of love was to marry a well-off girl, that the blessing of friendship was to help each other out of a financial tight spot, that wisdom was what the majority said it was, that passion was to give a speech, that courage was to risk being fined 10 rix-dollars, that cordiality was to say 'You're welcome' after a meal, and that the fear of God was to go to communion once a year. That's what I saw. And I laughed.

When we reach Kierkegaard's position of finding everything ludicrous, we enter into a nihilistic mood stemming from unsatisfactory answers to the question 'Why?'. In nihilism, there is no intrinsic meaning or value to life, and we are met with a sense of futility. The English rock band *The Godfathers* summed up the mood with their hit in the eighties, 'Birth, School, Work, Death': a great title for a nihilistic anthem (and a personal favourite).

Nietzsche saw the nihilistic state as pathological in that it mistakes a lack of meaning in old values as a lack of any meaning to life at all. Rather than being stuck with the depressing thought that life is meaningless, Nietzsche believed that nihilism should be seen as a necessary but *transitional* stage along the path to a life well lived.

Nietzsche's Solution: Active Nihilism, Amor Fati, and Becoming Who You Are

Nietzsche divided nihilism into two camps: a passive nihilism in which the individual takes a 'why bother?' attitude towards life, succumbing to a monotone, humdrum existence avoiding active engagement with the world; and an active nihilism in which a person consciously lets go of outmoded beliefs and creates new meaning in their life. For Nietzsche, such meaning came from the idea that a seed of unrealised potential lies within all of us, and our life's calling is to realise this potential, thus 'becoming who we are'.

Nietzsche emphasised that this journey requires strength and courage: it's not for the faint-hearted. It asks that we meet our fears and stretch beyond them. It also calls for us to step beyond the authority of others and develop an independent relationship with our own conscience. We need to turn to our 'inner law' from here on in, and trust that it will take us where we need to go.

The trouble early in the journey is that we haven't yet gone far enough to be free of self-doubt. In *The Tightrope Walker*, the taunting Jester represents society's 'shoulds' and 'oughts' that haunt us, telling us to get back with the program. The person who begins to think independently through actively reflecting on life is no longer akin to an animal (in Nietzsche's paradigm), but they are not yet what Nietzsche calls an 'overman' — a person who has achieved the balance between moralism (the slavish life of the herd) and nihilism (*nothing really matters*) — and so the path from one to the other involves some trepidation:

Man is a rope, tied between beast and overman — a rope over an abyss. A dangerous across, a dangerous on-the-way, a dangerous looking-back, a dangerous shuddering and stopping.

It is also true that the more we engage with the world in the process of expressing our potential, the more we will encounter setbacks and obstacles. We should embrace such challenges, says Nietzsche — saying 'yes' to *all* that comes our way — because every circumstance provides us with the opportunity for growth and can become a means of realising our potential:

My formula for greatness in a human being is amor fati: that one wants nothing to be different, not forward, not backward, not in all eternity. Not merely bear what is necessary, still less conceal it — all idealism is mendacity in the face of what is necessary — but love it.

Amor Fati — loving your fate — contains a radical acceptance of suffering, not as atonement, but as something that forces us to respond heroically and in so doing become 'healthier'. 'The great health' according to Nietzsche is that we are able to say 'yes' to all aspects of life, the 'good' and the 'ugly', what is fortuitous and what is tragic. To accept that all growth, all 'becoming', involves pain (just as our birth did), is the beginning of earthly heroism: 'The *heroic* man extols his existence by means of tragedy'. Amor Fati, therefore, is an ode to the human spirit, to the strength of the individual to endure and overcome.

Between the Atheist and the Martyr

Moralism encapsulates the overarching beliefs and values of the time, and for much of the Western world's history, that has included the morals of Christianity. For Neitzsche, Christianity embodies a philosophy of life-denial. In *The Anti-Christ*, he suggests that Christianity 'wages war' against passion, pride and sensuality, promoting self-sacrifice in the hope of happiness in an afterlife and in appeasement of a judgmental God.

In contrast, Nietzsche saw active nihilism as a philosophy of cheerfulness which says it's okay to enjoy your life; *this* life. This sentiment is reminiscent of the 2008 'Atheist Bus Campaign' in London where slogans such as 'There's probably no god. Now stop worrying and enjoy your life', adorned the sides of buses. The Atheist campaign was in response to evangelical advertisements with slogans such as 'When the son of man comes, will he find faith on the earth?'. And so, the battle was on — enjoy yourself/don't enjoy yourself; indulge yourself/don't indulge yourself — played out on the streets of metropolitan London.

The conflict between the nihilist and moralist can be framed as one between atheist and martyr, with each as a response to ideas about God's Will. This is expressed in the following passage from *A Course in Miracles*:

If, then, a mind believes that its will is different from His, it can only decide either that there is no God or that God's Will is fearful. The former accounts for the atheist and the latter for the martyr, who believes that God demands sacrifices (T-9.I.8:2-3).

The martyr aims to unite their will with God's, but they believe God's Will for them is to suffer. The atheist is wedded to their right to be happy and so takes the stance that God (whose Will calls for suffering) doesn't exist.

Either of these insane decisions will induce panic, because the atheist believes he is alone, and the martyr believes that God is crucifying him. Yet no one really wants either abandonment or retaliation, even though many may seek both (T-9.I.8:4-5).

The atheist will suffer from a fear of abandonment and a sense of loneliness; the martyr from a fear of retaliation and a generalised sense

66

of danger. The first case assumes that we are alone and so we'll feel *deprived*, the second that our passions are something to be negated and so we'll experience a sense of *sacrifice*. Yet both feelings of deprivation and sacrifice stem from having dissociated ourselves from Everything:

If truth demanded they give up the world, it would appear to them as if it asked the sacrifice of something that is real. Many have chosen to renounce the world while still believing its reality. And they have suffered from a sense of loss, and have not been released accordingly. Others have chosen nothing but the world, and they have suffered from a sense of loss still deeper, which they did not understand (W-155.4:1-4).

The answer lies between these opposite poles:

Between these paths there is another road that leads away from loss of every kind, for sacrifice and deprivation both are quickly left behind. This is the way appointed for you now (W-155.5:1-2).

Between moralism (God's Will calls for self-sacrifice) and atheism (there is no God. We're 'home alone' but can do more or less as we please) is the Course's answer, expressed in lessons 101 and 102 respectively: 'God's Will for me is perfect happiness'; and 'I share God's Will for happiness for me'. In other words, we do have a right to be happy (God's Will), and we're not alone (there is a God and we share His Will).

The Issue of Transcendence

While Nietzsche and *A Course in Miracles* share in the idea that we must question the values handed down to us in order to realise our potential, they differ significantly on what that potential is. For Nietzsche, the heroic individual is one who embraces the idea of becoming something great, and moves forward (sometimes selfishly and with a lust for power) in order to achieve 'excellence'. In contrast, the Course says that *nothing in this world* — not even striving for greatness, gladly enduring suffering to achieve our worldly ambitions — will satisfy us. This is because who we are *isn't of this world*. Nietzsche saw life as a means of *constructing* a self; *A Course in Miracles* sees life as a means of *remembering* who we are.

The Course's path to remembrance is to heal our self-concept from a sinful, shameful, separated self, full of contradictions and at war within and without, to an innocent, whole Self at one with God and each other. Forgiveness is the way we heal, and is the reflection in this world of God's Will for us. It is via the process of forgiveness that we let go of our mistaken belief in separation and the shame and guilt associated with it.

Anything we feel guilty for, we project out and judge harshly in others, then identify with the opposite. If I feel guilty for my passionate nature, for example, I'll attack passionate displays in others, and overcompensate for what I have secretly judged harshly in myself by adopting a more 'moralistic' position. Through the process of forgiveness, as I let go of my judgement of someone for their unruly behaviour, I free myself from the chains of my own guilt and shame, and so will begin to express more of a balanced nature.

Through forgiveness, our passions ('atheistic' nature) and our sense of proportion and propriety ('moralistic' nature) assume their most harmonious relationship because neither is at war with the other, trying to assume dominance. In other words, we don't have to negate one in order to express the other. Through forgiveness, the positive aspects of both — vitality (instead of destructiveness: nihilism) and containment (instead of restriction: moralism) — enjoy a *complementary* relationship in which a third thing — wholeness — is experienced.

The difficulty for Nietzsche, was that there was no transcendent aspect to existence; no Self beyond the body to aid in reconciling what is contradictory in us. Trusting in our own strength means that we have made the ego thought system real, and must therefore identify with fear and vulnerability. While Nietzsche rallied against weakness, his emphasis on the power of the human will to achieve worldly greatness meant that his was a philosophy whose goal was littleness and whose method involved making oneself weak:

You always choose between your weakness and the strength of Christ in you (T-31.VIII.2:3).

In adopting the position that heroic excellence was 'the measure of a man', Nietzsche placed himself (and everyone else) under just as harsh a judgemental system as the moralist righteously affirming what is 'good' and 'evil'. I find it ironic that shortly before Nietzsche suffered a psychotic break, he rushed up to a horse being mercilessly whipped in a town square, then reached his arms around the horse's neck and wept. The insistence on worldly excellence is indeed a harsh taskmaster, and perhaps Nietzsche felt acutely the unkindness of his own unrelenting philosophy at that time of his life. *Isn't it enough to just 'be'?*

A *Course in Miracles* helps us see that we 'need do nothing' (T-18.VII.5:5) for our salvation, because God wants us to be happy, and we share in His Will, remaining connected to Him. In order to express who we are in respect to our personality (to be 'authentic') means to move beyond the psychological extremes of moralism and nihilism, the martyr and the atheist. Since the memory of our unity with God, as expressed in the symbol of the Holy Spirit, undoes our belief in separation, being receptive to it gives us the necessary strength to face the shame and guilt expressed in our extreme stance.

In part two of this post we'll continue to explore Nietzsche's thoughts on opposites. In particular we'll look at his theory of art based on the Greek gods Apollo and Dionysus, and its relevance to the notion of becoming who we are.

13

The Tightrope Walker: Part Two

Nietzsche saw the overman as a free-thinker, an 'artist' — not someone who lives a passive life simply in pursuit of pleasure or what they can get, but who has a need to be creative. Creativity isn't limited to producing a work of art such as a sonnet or a painting, but in living a life that is truly our own: we don't try to imitate others or unthinkingly adhere to what the majority approves of.

The creative life, for Nietzsche, is one that expresses active nihilism: we let go of traditional expectations that don't satisfy our need for meaning, and yet don't fall into a state of inertia because we turn to another source for inspiration — our inner world — in pursuit of excellence. That inner world, according to Nietzsche, contains Dionysian and Apollonian characteristics.

Dionysus and Apollo: The Artist Within

Dionysus (also known as Bacchus) was the ancient Greek God of ecstasy and wine. He was known as 'the liberator' for his ability to take us out of the chains of habit – he had intoxicating powers to aid self-forgetting, often in a frenzy of unbridled passion and excess. Dionysus also represents disorder, chaos, vitality, irrationality, instinct and is associated with hedonism, a lack of discipline, and breaking boundaries. He is, therefore, somewhat of a mascot for the nihilistic position in that he isn't restricted by thoughts of consequence or approval. He also represents tragedy (as well as ecstasy) — both pleasure and pain, joy and sorrow — and to stand in a Dionysian relationship to life is to embrace whatever comes your way, much in the spirit of Nietzsche's Amor Fati.

In contrast, Apollonian qualities are more or less aligned with moralism. Apollo represents the constraining, moderating aspect of the psyche: reason, order, form, structure, and self-awareness — where the Dionysian influence causes us to lose ourselves in wild abandon, measured restraint gives us a sense of self. Dionysus was the god of drink, music, and self-forgetting; Apollo the god of culture, order, harmony and restraint. Sigmund Freud, the father of psychoanalysis, was influenced by Nietzsche's writing, and his concept of the id and superego loosely parallel Nietzsche's distinction between the Dionysian (id/instinctual) and the Apollonian (superego/inner parent).

Nietzsche was fascinated by the art of ancient Greece. He saw the Apollonian spirit reflected in the order of Greek architecture, and the Dionysian spirit expressed through music and dance. When the Apollonian and Dionysian worked perfectly together, they formed 'tragedies', or dramatic works which evoked a sense of communal participation amongst the audience, along with an apprehension of the common human experience – something Nietzsche valued highly.

Nietzsche concluded that artists must employ both a Dionysian and Apollonian spirit to create a work of art. His focus, however, was often on the detrimental effects of a tightly-held moralism in the equation: with its emphasis on reining in the passions, moralism is the great enemy of creativity — it causes us to neglect our Dionysian nature, and so we cannot be a free spirit, an 'artist'. And as often was the case, Nietzsche augmented his argument with references to the 'life-denying' aspects of Christianity : 'A Christian who is at the same time an artist does not exist...' (*Twilight of the Idols*). In *The Anti-Christ*, he makes it clear that the puritanical aspects of Christianity stifle creativity by making us impotent:

The Church combats the passions with excision in every sense of the word; its practice, its 'cure' is castration... But to attack the passions at their roots means to attack life at its roots; the practice of the Church is hostile to life...

The saint in whom God takes pleasure is the ideal castrate.

In *The Birth of Tragedy*, Nietzsche says we need a level of psychological 'intoxication' for any sort of creation to exist, and such intoxication comes from our Dionysian nature. It is that which moves us to into action beyond any conscious attempt to try and create something new. In this I'm reminded of the poet Charles Bukowski's advice to writers: *Don't try.* Bukowski didn't mean that we should be lazy, apathetic, or even despondent, but that we shouldn't use our intellect, or 'Apollonian' nature, to try and muscle our way into a creative work or get it done. We should allow space for inspiration to meet us rather than try and make something happen:

You don't try. That's very important: "not" to try, either for Cadillacs, creation or immortality. You wait, and if nothing happens, you wait some more. It's like a bug high on the wall. You wait for it to come to you.

When the bug is close enough for you to reach out to it is when your Apollonian nature can kick-in to channel the inspiration into form and get the job done. For Nietzsche, all art depends on the opposing forces of the Dionysian and Apollonian, 'stimulating and provoking one another... until by a miracle of the Helenic 'Will', they appear paired and, in this pairing, finally engender a work of art that is Dionysiac and Apollonian in equal measure'. Without the Dionysian, what is produced would be sterile and have no 'music' to it, and without the Apollonian, there would be no way to channel what comes forth from our inner world into a comprehensible form that can be shared.

Becoming an Adult

Nietzsche viewed the overman (the person who has courageously accepted the task of becoming who they are) as an artist. In becoming ourselves, we need to work towards expressing both the Dionysian and Apollonian aspects of our nature, in our own unique way, through our calling.

Becoming who you are also means becoming an adult, no longer identifying yourself primarily as a child of your parents. Very often, the contrast between the Dionysian and the Apollonian is represented clearly in our parents. One, for example, might be loud and passionate, prone to emotional highs and lows, while the other is cooler and predictable in contrast, offering a more tranquil and measured affection. One might be the 'big spender', the other the diligent saver; one an exhibitionist, the other more reserved; one irrational and irresponsible, the other thoughtful and considerate.

Households with this sort of dynamic between parents (and all households have it in some measure) play out the conflict that is within everyone. At times the Dionysian individual can display a dangerous emotionality (extreme and chaotic); at times the Apollonian parent can appear austere and distant. How a child learns to navigate the extremes within themselves is influenced by seeing them played out externally in the family unit; the centre of their orbit. Just as art might be produced by the Dionysian and Apollonian 'stimulating and provoking each other', a relationship between parents can become the setting for intense drama. Rarely, however, does the interaction lead to the embodiment of a 'pairing' within each individual.

To become an adult, we need to be aware of these extremes within us and learn to navigate them on our own terms. This involves letting go of lessons learnt from our parents regarding passion on the one hand, and self-control on the other: it's likely that we aligned ourselves more with one parent, for example, at the cost of embodying our Dionysian or Apollonian nature. And of course, when we emphasise differences amongst people, we also make value judgements regarding good and evil, victim and victimizer.

We will relive these conflicts with our partners, and with authority figures such as bosses, therapists, the taxation department and teachers. Forgiveness of the historical context of our 'lopsidedness' is how we clear the way to tune in to our own inner, loving Authority, letting it become our new centre as we detach from the past. As Carl Jung said in *Symbols of Transformation,* our wellbeing depends on developing such a relationship with our own centre:

All the libido [energy] that was tied up in family bonds must be withdrawn from the narrower circle into the larger one, because the psychic health of the adult individual, who in childhood was a mere particle revolving in a rotary system, demands that he should himself become the centre of a new system.

When we sense our opposite within and that it's okay to express it (it's no longer fearful to us) we can experience a sense of emancipation, freedom, joy, and abundance. What we have judged harshly in ourselves (and consequently in others) is no longer seen as dangerous (Dionysian), or sacrificial (Apollonian), and so we are able to express our wholeness. In repressing this other side of ourselves, we have been holding ourselves back, restricting our movements and limiting our ability to 'play'. And as

Jung says in *The Archetypes of the Collective Unconscious*, the recognition of this lost aspect, not as a fiend but a friend, also ushers in a greater capacity to love, because the wholeness of the personality is a reflection of the abundance of the 'greater personality', the Self: 'the recognition of a greater personality seems to burst an iron ring round the heart'.

Few Choose to Listen

The path to reconciling these opposites within us is very challenging. This is because we over-identified with one at the expense of the other, believing this would keep us safe. Our predominantly Dionysian or Apollonian (nihilistic or moralistic) attitude is really a defence against anxiety, and will involve habitual ways of thinking and behaving that have become so ingrained that we mistake them for our character. To begin to address them is therefore to face the dismantling of a lifetime's work. We have become so attached to who we think we are, that the process of letting go will be painful, *very* painful, because of our resistance.

Letting go of our defences also requires that we face the guilt and shame we tried to hide beneath them. This is why myths often involve the hero having to move through a dark and menacing subterranean underworld; symbolic of the shame and guilt we've been afraid to face.

Closely tied to our resistance to losing these defences is our reluctance to let go of our ego. We simply don't trust that we'll be better off without it. If, through the process of forgiveness, we're able to loosen our hold on our defences thus becoming more balanced, we're approaching the earthly reflection of the wholeness of our Self. This will mean that we're able to move more 'wholeheartedly' in a particular direction, fulfilling our life's work — we now have the Dionysian and Apollonian aspects of our personality available to fully collaborate in the pursuit of a creative life. The need to sacrifice (moralism) won't restrict us heavy-handedly, nor will a nihilistic mood fight against the discipline required to channel inspiration or meet a long-range goal.

Though the rewards of living a creative life are significant, few choose to listen to the call for integration. Life then takes on a listless hue, like we're just passing time, going through the motions, or 'sitting in God's waiting room'. All of us, on some level and at some stage, are tempted to ignore the call, not only because of the challenges involved, but so that we can hold onto our grievances (wedded to our chosen defences), and through our misery put certain others to shame – aren't they the reason we can't seem to get on our feet/sustain a relationship/get along with our kids?

The first step to 'knowing ourselves' and embodying our personality is to become aware of the larger context of our lives. The Course's myth describes how a fear of abandonment and retribution stem from a belief in separation — from our Source and each other. We fear abandonment for falling short of some ideal (shame-anxiety) because God didn't give us the special favour we demanded, and we fear retribution for having gone our own way (guilt-anxiety), establishing our 'independence'.

The moralist represents the fear of retribution and the nihilist the fear of abandonment, and when it comes to living a creative life, both will put on the breaks, albeit for different reasons. The passive nihilist isn't sure there will be a satisfactory reward (enough pleasure through recognition), the moralist isn't sure their creativity (potency and individuality) won't meet with a disastrous end. For example, in an interview (*One Plus One*, ABC television) with Tom Keneally, author of *Schindler's Ark*, Keneally spoke of the mental health issues that plagued him when writing a book. His explanation was that the creative act of writing is like Prometheus stealing the power of fire from the gods, and so the ensuing inner turmoil is retribution. This is of course a metaphor, but illustrates the kind of symbolic language active in the unconscious, and our fears surrounding living a creative life.

The ontological, or mythical, component of our fear is important to consider because it gives us an appreciation of the magnitude of the task. We are, ultimately, afraid of God, and so moving beyond our fears requires us to address our imagined relationship to Him. Unlike Nietzsche's assertion that the pairing of the Dionysian and Apollonian within is achieved through 'a miracle of the Helenic [human] "Will"', the Course affirms that we connect with the wholeness of our Self (thus transcending all opposites and fear) when we share in God's Will, and we do this by practicing forgiveness. It's through listening to the Holy Spirit that we rise above the fear of retribution and abandonment, because our creativity is then the result of a collaboration with our Inner Teacher. It's also with the Holy Spirit's help that we no-longer perceive the apparent differences between us — atheist, martyr, impulsive, restrained — as any big deal, and whenever this is our experience, we can be sure we are being who we are.

14

Mind the Gap

'I had two longings and one was fighting the other. I wanted to be loved and I wanted to be always alone.'

These are the words of Antoinette Cosway, the protagonist in Jean Rhys's novel *Wide Sargasso Sea*. The book is a prequel of sorts to Charlotte Bronte's *Jane Eyre*, providing a back-story to the life of Mr. Rochester's first wife (spoiler alert — the one secretly locked away upstairs).

The sentiment is a common one: we wish for the security, warmth and companionship of an intimate relationship, yet they can also be stressful so we'd prefer to be alone. The German philosopher Arthur Schopenhauer came up with the following story about porcupines as a metaphor for this conflict:

One cold winter's day, a number of porcupines huddled together quite closely in order through their mutual warmth to prevent themselves from being frozen. But they soon felt the effect of their quills on one another, which made them again move apart. Now when the need for warmth once more brought them together, the drawback of the quills was repeated so that they were tossed between two evils, until they had discovered the proper distance from which they could best tolerate one another.

Schopenhauer then drew an analogy between the porcupines and people; between the quills and what we find objectionable about others:

Thus the need for society which springs from the emptiness and monotony of men's lives, drives them together; but their many unpleasant and repulsive qualities and insufferable drawbacks once more drive them apart. The mean distance which they finally discover, and which enables them to endure being together, is politeness and good manners... By virtue thereof, it is true that the need for mutual warmth will be only imperfectly satisfied, but, on the other hand, the prick of the quills won't be felt.

A Qualified Entente

In terms of *A Course in Miracles,* our wish to be a separate, autonomous being is symbolically expressed in the gap between bodies. The real gap, however, is in our minds where the thought of separation lies, but, identifying with the ego, we're not aware of this and seek to relieve loneliness by joining with other bodies: all relationships that the ego establishes are used to protect us from our loneliness. We also establish them so we can project out our guilt, thereby getting rid of it (or so we think):

In their angry alliances, born of the fear of loneliness and yet dedicated to the continuance of loneliness, each seeks relief from guilt by increasing it in the other. For each believes that this decreases guilt in him. The other seems always to be attacking and wounding him, perhaps in little ways, perhaps 'unconsciously,' yet never without demand of sacrifice (T-15.VII.9:3-5).

However, as long as we identify as a body (at the mercy of things it cannot control, rather than as a mind that can choose to see things differently) we are identifying with the thought of separation and so *nothing* will suffice as a substitute for the comfort of Everything. The Course also points out that as long as we believe being with another body will get rid of our loneliness, we will be invested in perceiving people as bodies, which means we will only see the foibles of their ego (rather than calls for help) and make them into a big deal:

As long as you believe that to be with a body is companionship, you will be compelled to attempt to keep your brother in his body, held there by guilt. And you will see safety in guilt and danger in communication (T-15.VII.12:2-3).

Though we blame our annoyance on someone's characteristics or behaviour (their 'quills'), the Course points out that our annoyance is *purposive*. Indeed, both parties in the equation have shared in a secret treaty, or 'entente', in which their egos agreed to maintain their illusion of separateness:

Let him come close to you, and you jumped back; as you approached, did he but instantly withdraw. A cautious friendship, and limited in scope and carefully restricted in amount, became the treaty that you had made with him. Thus you and your brother but shared a qualified entente, in which a clause of separation was a point you both agreed to keep intact (T-29.I.3:7-9).

We appear to be 'friends' while we meet each other's special needs — for approval, or security — but when these needs aren't met, and when our ego wants to affirm itself, we will whip out the contract in which we both agreed to maintain our distance. And while we each feel victimised by the other, our egos are mutually satisfied with the situation: we have reinforced our identity as a body that needs another body to treat us in a certain way to have peace. This, to the ego, is a job well done.

So, while we think we want love, we have a need to emphasise our differences, our separateness. There is, therefore, no love without ambivalence in this world:

You do not see how limited and weak is your allegiance [to love], and how frequently you have demanded that love go away, and leave you quietly alone in 'peace.' (T-29.I.7:5).

We are conflicted about love, and about each other, because we have a split mind: we want to maintain our identity as a separate, special self, but we also want to be done with the charade and go Home. In this I'm reminded of a recurring dream in which I'm trying to get home but keep missing public transport connections. In variations of the dream I'm looking for my mobile phone to call someone (usually someone close to me) but can't find it, or can't physically dial their number or remember it. Either way, the dream draws a parallel between re-establishing communication with a particular person (through forgiveness/not emphasising the 'slings and arrows') and returning Home.

Our real fear isn't of future loss or pain, but of communication, because in communion there is no 'I' (which in practical terms means there's no neediness):

Future loss is not your fear.   But present joining is your dread (T-26.VIII.4:3-4).

We have a *need* to see separate interests — to push others away — when the threat of communication looms. That's why the Course refers to the *'temptation* to perceive [ourselves] unfairly treated' (T-26.X.4:1). The path forward is to look at this need and not judge it, remembering that we all share in the same ego thought system and the same Self. This is how we accept our sameness; our unity. Our job is simply to be willing to let go of our insistence that we are right, that we are different, that our peace has been destroyed by others. This small willingness, this 'nod to God', is all we need for the perceived gap to be healed by the Holy Spirit:

Your willingness to let illusions go is all the Healer of God's Son requires. He will place the miracle of healing where the seeds of sickness were. And there will be no loss, but only gain (T-28.V.10:8-10).

15

One or the Other

Several years ago, I saw a television program about children growing up in different postcodes — families from affluent areas were contrasted with those from some of the most poverty-stricken. One episode was about parents with a teenage boy, located in an exclusive inner suburb of Sydney, and a teenage girl growing up in a remote town with few job opportunities.

The girl was one of many children in her family, her mother had died, and her father drove for hours to attend work out of town. This left her (as the eldest child) to help look after her siblings. Little attention was given to her education, preferences, possible talents or interests — all of which were sacrificed due to the time constraints on her father, and the need to assist in the running of the household. She appeared aimless in her free time, often wandering the streets with her smartphone looking for free Wi-Fi, and her biggest ambition was to get married and own a Toyota Landcruiser.

In contrast, the teenage boy from Sydney had 'the world at his feet'. His mother acted as his manager; nurturing his passion for the theatre and his goal of performing Shakespeare one day in London. He enjoyed various organised extra-curricular activities and spoke of his busy, full, and exciting life and was intoxicated with the possibilities he imagined for his future. He was the centre of his parents' world and it was clear that his mother sacrificed a great deal of time and energy to help him make the most of his talents.

In another program (*Australian Story*, ABC television), Steven McRae, a principle ballet dancer for a dance company in London, spoke of how much his working-class parents had sacrificed for him to get where he was. His family, back in Australia, lamented that they don't speak to or visit him as often as they'd like, and they seldom see him perform or get to experience his success first hand.

Sacrifice: The Ego's Foundation

It is little wonder that the world, and our lives, are full of examples of sacrifice. The world itself was made from the thought of 'one or the other' — from the idea that God's oneness had to be sacrificed in order for us to have our autonomy. This wish for a separate identity is the essence of the ego, and from a thought of sacrifice came a world in which the theme of sacrifice pervades absolutely every encounter: if you are to gain, someone else must go without; if you are to win, someone else must lose. Just think of the haggling that goes with buying a car, the negotiations between siblings over who will take out the garbage, or the surge of adrenaline we experience upon sight of an empty space in a busy parking lot ('*Quick, there's one!*').

We do a lot of bargaining to sacrifice as little as possible to get what we want, but sacrifice we do, whether it be time, money, or attention. All of these instances of sacrifice relate to ourselves as bodies: time, money, attention, mean nothing to spirit; to our *Self*. Likewise, *A Course in Miracles* points out that the real sacrifice occurs when we try and find happiness in the things of the world thereby sacrificing awareness of our wholeness:

It takes great learning both to realize and to accept the fact that the world has nothing to give... There is no sacrifice in the world's terms that does not involve the body. Think a while about what the world calls sacrifice. Power, fame, money, physical pleasure; who is the 'hero' to whom all these things belong? Could they mean anything except to a body?... By seeking after such things the mind associates itself with the body, obscuring its Identity and losing sight of what it really is (M-13.2:1, 4-7, 9).

Gratitude for what the world gives us is part of the 'one-or-the-other' mentality because it is based on what we have or don't have on the level of form. Many people, for example, say grace before a meal, in thanks for the food before them. But how can this not remind us that there are people who are without food, with apparently less to be thankful for?

Gratitude is a lesson hard to learn for those who look upon the world amiss. The most that they can do is see themselves as better off than others. And they try to be content because another seems to suffer more than they. How pitiful and deprecating are such thoughts! For who has cause for thanks while others have less cause? And who could suffer less because he sees another suffer more? (W-195.1:1-6).

Because we can't all have the same things, or the same external experiences, being thankful for things of the world emphasises a 'have and have-not' mentality. We can't help but feel guilty if others appear to have it worse, or feel deprived if they seem to have it better. And when it comes to externals, how can we judge what is best for all concerned in the greater scheme of things? Our circumstances and 'hits and misses' on the level of form are neutral — our *interpretations*, however, speak to the teacher (the ego or the Holy Spirit) with whom we have chosen to look at them, and this will influence how we feel.

Gratitude, then, is an expression of love that comes from knowing that despite all that goes on around us, or 'to' us (both the 'good' and the 'bad'), we can still be at peace because of Who we are and Who is with us. This is what the Course calls the 'Atonement' principle — that despite all seeming evidence to the contrary, we haven't sacrificed oneness, but remain as God created us, whole and in need of nothing to be at peace:

Your gratitude is due to Him alone Who made all cause of sorrow disappear throughout the world...

We have been given everything. If we refuse to recognize it, we are not entitled therefore to our bitterness... Gratitude becomes the single thought we substitute for these insane perceptions. God has cared for us, and calls us Son. Can there be more than this? (W-195.1:7;2:1-6).

Being grateful for Who we are is indirectly achieved by being willing to see all that goes on in our lives as an opportunity to practice forgiveness. Through forgiveness and the healing of our unworthy self-concept, we open the door to awareness of our innocent Self, and gratitude is a natural result. We don't, therefore, have gratitude for what we get (the ego is all about *getting* because it based on a belief in scarcity) but for Who we are, and have always been:

But to receive is to accept, not to get. It is impossible not to have, but it is possible not to know you have (T-9.II.11:5-6).

Sacrifice, Guilt, and Autonomy

Again, we don't know we 'have' because we believe we sacrificed God's oneness for our individual existence, our autonomy, and in doing so sacrificed Everything for something that can never measure up. We then project our guilt for depriving ourselves onto others, including God, believing that they are depriving us of love/comfort/joy/security.

If only they would be fair and give us our due. We also protect ourselves from God's punishment for our insubordination by showing Him how good we are by sacrificing ourselves for others.

Indeed, the Bible is full of examples in which a willingness to sacrifice our happiness is a true test of our allegiance to God. In Genesis, for example, God decides to test Abraham by telling him to kill his only son, Isaac, whom he loved very much, as a sacrifice. Abraham obediently fetched Isaac and took him to the top of a mountain and bound him with rope to an altar. When Abraham lifted his knife to kill Isaac, an angel told him not to kill his son — that God was satisfied with his allegiance and would reward him.

This story illustrates how the ego thought system operates. We believe that we demonstrate our 'love' by giving up things for the beloved, but we are really hoping that through our sacrifice we are pleasing God. Parents, or other authority-figures, such as bosses, can sometimes play this godlike game with their children, employees, or 'underlings'. I remember as a child sitting in front of the television with my siblings, comfortably watching a favourite program, and my father would say from his chair, 'Who will get up and make me a cup of coffee?'. Our enjoyment would instantly cease as we all sat frozen and silent. None of us wanted to get up, but we knew one of us would have to. As soon as someone relented and went to make dad's coffee you'd hear in an ominous tone, 'Thank you ____. Now I know who would make a coffee for me,' and we all knew what he meant by that!

Not only do we believe we need to sacrifice to please God and protect ourselves from Him, we believe we need to sacrifice our happiness to get the love we need from others. Our sacrifice can also be an attack, because through our suffering we point to the object of our sacrifice as the cause of our pain/anger/resentment/lack of fulfillment. The ballet dancer, Steven McRae, for example, spoke of his guilt for choosing his career over his family — for being the object of his parents' sacrifice —

and that perhaps they had sacrificed too much for him.

Form Versus Content

So, how do we avoid sacrifice? As mentioned earlier, sacrifice is only relevant to bodies, and on that level, it can't be avoided. Some will gain on the level of form, and some will lose; some will get more and some will get less. What matters is the content of an interaction — the ideas we are reinforcing by the way we perceive things. While our body might give something tangible to someone, what counts is the thought that goes along with it. Are we giving to get?— security? affection? attention? salvation? In every encounter, we are teaching what we are, and the Course reminds us that if we share an idea, we strengthen it:

If you share a physical possession, you do divide its ownership. If you share an idea, however, you do not lessen it. All of it is still yours although all of it has been given away... If you can accept the concept that the world is one of ideas, the whole belief in the false association the ego makes between giving and losing is gone (T-5.I.1:10-12, 14).

The idea we want to teach is that despite separate interests on the level of form, we have a shared interest in fulfilling our one need — to know of our holiness. And if we first join with Jesus, the Holy Spirit, or whatever symbol of non-judgemental love appeals to us, then we are joined with everyone in that love, and we have everything along with everyone else.

Salvation is rebirth of the idea no one can lose for anyone to gain. And everyone must gain, if anyone would be a gainer. Here is sanity restored. And on this single rock of truth can faith in God's eternal saneness rest in perfect confidence and perfect peace (T-25.VII.12).

The end of sacrifice therefore comes with realising we're not alone; that within our mind is an 'appointed friend' whose presence answers everyone's shared need. When we connect with that abstract presence or memory of love and wholeness, we won't feel a need to sacrifice for others, or demand that they sacrifice for us. We will simply do whatever we feel to do on the level of form — whether that looks like sacrifice or not — and remain peaceful in the process. As always, it's not *what* we do but *who* we do it with that counts, and when we do things with the Holy Spirit as our teacher, everyone gains.

About the Author

Stephanie Panayi has worked as a Rolfer™ and counsellor, graduating from the Rolf Institute® (USA and Brazil) in 1998, and from Swinburne University (Australia) with a degree is psychology and psychophysiology, in 2004. A student of *A Course in Miracles* for twenty years, Stephanie integrated its principles within her professional practice and enjoys writing from a Course perspective.

Also by Stephanie Panayi

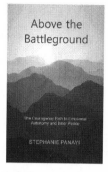

Above the Battleground: The Courageous Path to Emotional Autonomy and Inner Peace
'I wish I hadn't got so upset!'. These words are familiar to all of us. Why do we go on automatic pilot when we feel rejected or unfairly treated, retaliating with an outburst that we later regret? And why are there curious similarities in the course of our relationships with friends, partners, and jobs?

Above the Battleground explores the origins of our most intense emotional needs and how they send us into self-defeating battles to have them met. Using psychological theory, principles from *A Course in Miracles*, and examples from the author's clinical experience, *Above the Battleground* provides a unique take on the origins of our deepest insecurities along with a way to rise above them to achieve a sense of security, happiness and peace.

Made in the USA
Middletown, DE
24 November 2020